86387
Johnson

PR
4754
.J58

DATE DUE

MAY 9 '94			
MR 01 '01			

DEMCO 38-297

True Correspondence

True Correspondence
A Phenomenology of Thomas Hardy's Novels

Bruce Johnson

A Florida State University Book
University Presses of Florida
Tallahassee

Library of Congress Cataloging in Publication Data

Johnson, Bruce, 1933–
  True correspondence, a phenomenology of
Thomas Hardy's novels.

  "A Florida State University book."
  Includes bibliographical references and index.
  1. Hardy, Thomas, 1840–1928—Criticism and in-
terpretation. 2. Phenomenology and literature.
I. Title.
PR4754.J58   1983   823'.8   83–3456
ISBN 0-8130-0764-X

University Presses of Florida, the publisher of scholarly and creative works for Florida's state
university system, operates under the policies adopted by the Board of Regents. Its offices are
located at 15 NW 15th Street, Gainesville, FL 32603.
  Works published by University Presses of Florida are evaluated and selected for publication, after being reviewed by referees both within and outside of the state's university system, by a faculty editorial committee of any one of Florida's nine public universities.

Contents

Acknowledgments

My thanks to the following publishers for permission to use copyrighted materials:

The University of California Press for permission to reprint in revised form the article " 'The Perfection of Species' and Hardy's Tess," which originally appeared in *Nature and the Victorian Imagination*, edited by U. C. Knoepflmacher and G. B. Tennyson (© 1977 by The Regents of the University of California).

Bobbs-Merrill for permission to quote from *Jude the Obscure*, edited by F. R. Southerington (© Bobbs-Merrill, 1972).

W. W. Norton & Company, Inc., for permission to quote from *Tess of the d'Urbervilles* by Thomas Hardy, A Norton Critical Edition, edited by Scott Elledge. By permission of W. W. Norton & Company, Inc. (© 1979, 1965 by W. W. Norton & Company, Inc.).

This study of Thomas Hardy was begun during a Senior NEH Fellowship, and I wish to acknowledge the help of the National Endowment for the Humanities.

For Abe

Introduction

The student of literature who wants to experience the true spirit of phe-nomenology would do well to go directly to the source and to avoid ini-tially the inheritors of Edmund Husserl's methods, men such as Gaston Bachelard and Jean-Paul Sartre, or contemporary American literary critics such as J. Hillis Miller and Edward Said. I say this not because these inheri-tors are less reputable than the master; after all, in their application of phe-nomenological method to literary texts, all four of these critics and many others attempt something that did not much interest Husserl.[1] I suggest a return to the text of Husserl himself because the essential spirit of phe-nomenological inquiry seems often to have been overshadowed by the complex method he left to his students and to philosophers such as Hei-degger. The difficult sequence of "reductions," for instance, seems rather quickly to have supplanted in the minds of his students the original poetic insight of the *epokhē*, the "abstention."

In this brief introduction, I have no intention of sorting out the diffi-culties of *Ideen zu einer reinen Phänomenologie und phänomenologischen Philosophie*, published in 1913 and subsequently called simply *Ideen*, or *Ideas*.[2] It does seem to me, however, that if we set aside the earlier and less confident *Logical Investigations* (1900–1901), *Ideas* cries out for inter-pretation as a period piece, as an eloquent cultural artifact more expressive of 1913, of that long golden autumn before the winter of "world" war, than many an Edwardian novel or Futurist painting. In this waning light the phenomenological method can be seen as the last passionate defense of pure subjectivity against the deluge of logical positivism. From a French or English point of view, no doubt Husserl's defense of subjectivity seemed typically Germanic, with its claims of rigor, its incredibly involuted syn-tax, and finally its claim of changing impressions into essences.

My emphasis, however, is that the phenomenological method described in *Ideas* (particularly the *epokhē*, the bracketing, abstention, or disconnec-tion) emerges from the waning of the nineteenth century and the first dec-ade or so of the twentieth (to 1913), from a time which nurtured many of the transitionally modern attitudes of Thomas Hardy. The idea of the *ep-okhē* is so typically late Victorian that we might on another occasion want to compare it with the peculiar abstention of James Joyce that finds the author standing in the wings paring his fingernails, or with the disappearance of the author in general, or even with the idea of the objective correlative. It is no mere accident that all these putative abstentions are characteristic of early modernism. The goal in all of them carries the flavor of Husserl's admonition: "Zu den Sachen selbst," to the things themselves!

Like most early moderns, Husserl begins with the problem of identifying the *unique* quality of consciousness and argues that we can only discover the essence of pure consciousness through applying the *epokhē* to the so-called natural attitude (*Ideas*, 102–3): when we "bracket" the world we not only suspend all questions of "being" ("completely bars me from using any judgment of spatio-temporal existence," 100) but enter "a primordial form of apprehension" (103) where the only unimpeachable evidence is wholly subjective, that this or that is the way something seemed to me. The daydream and other deliberately various and conscious flights of imagination become a surer entrance and guide to the realm of essences than the most highly ordered system or theory. We attempt to experience the world free of theory in anticipation of discovering true essences.

This deliberate encouragement of the reader's impression is what frightens most American literary critics who are trained in the New Criticism and never far from believing in some version of E. D. Hirsch's "objective interpretation." It constitutes, however, no part of my phenomenological approach to the novels of Thomas Hardy. My sense, rather, is that both Husserl and Hardy emerge from late-Victorian contexts that, for whatever reason, encourage "a primordial form of apprehension," a new humility allowing glimpses under the "nets" of theory and preconception, and that the best phenomenological approach to Hardy is precisely a reconstruction of those original contexts and of that original spirit shared by both men. The very useful metaphor of the nets comes from Iris Murdoch's first novel, *Under the Net* (1954), written while she was studying the phenomenology of both Sartre and Wittgenstein, and from one of the characters in the novel, Hugo Belfounder, who brilliantly suggests Wittgenstein's preoccupation with the linguistic screens that determine so much of our perception.

Certainly the most important feature of my critical method in this study is to reconstruct Hardy's attempt at eluding the most apparently unavoidable categories of perception, especially those that separate the world into human and nonhuman. Hardy's familiarity with the pastoral had early persuaded him that the most "primordial form of apprehension" did not preserve this distinction and, quite the contrary, depended on its dissolution. The whole late-Victorian and early modern period, from the 1880s to the advent of the Great War, sought in disciplines apparently as disparate as anthropology and modern poetry to pass behind and before assumptions that to many Victorians had seemed irreducibly fundamental. Behind Christianity lay Jesse Weston's and James Frazer's description of the Fisher King and the fertility cults; behind hysterical symptoms lay the repressed traumas of early childhood, and so on.

The reader may detect a similar passion for penetrating to the *ur-alt* in most disciplines of the period. The maneuver seems to me definitive of early modernism. For Hardy, as for Husserl, the modern world seemed to demand new ways of perceiving that were most new because most primordial. I do not, in short, apply my own version of phenomenology to Hardy, but attempt to discover the late-Victorian, early modern phenomenological bias that both writers share because of enormous cultural forces as yet imperfectly understood by historians of either philosophy or fiction. Phenomenology is originally a creature of 1880–1913, not of 1945–1982. It should not be at all surprising to find Hardy and Husserl using similar tactics to avoid the nets.

Most of the writers who produced the great systematic holy books of early modernism—those prodigiously cosmic wakes and fantasias and visions—were interested, as D. H. Lawrence said, in seeing the "nonhuman" in human character, in breaking old Victorian illusions of coherent, cohesive ego that had informed the novel even when most it showed fragmentation in a David Copperfield or a Pip or a Jane Eyre. For Yeats, this ego-shattering meant introducing a metaphor of human identity in which consciousness becomes like an actor who joins the Commedia dell'Arte and is forced to create an identity among the competing demands of the script, the director, the actor's own reading, the tradition of the company, and the larger aesthetic tradition.[3] As Wylie Sypher sees the development, easy conceptions of human self were persistently undercut and ultimately all but lost, as they were later to be visually depicted in the strangely eroded figures of Giacommeti or even more vividly in the graphics and paintings of Dubuffet.[4] Perhaps the epitome of the whole development lies in Sartre's phenomenology of consciousness in *Being and Nothingness*, where consciousness's mode of being—its "nature" we might say, if that ancient word had not been entirely decentered—is to go about not-being, bringing nothing-ness into the world, no consciousness ever at one with an identity.

Darwin and the whole current of new scientific awareness sweeping him into place saw man as the result of impersonal processes that had made all nature, not the result of unique, divine intentions that he inherit or dominate anything. If the presiding emotion of the anthropocentric view of the cosmos was pride or egotism—or at least the Christian hope of inheriting—the controlling emotion of the new orientation must come close to the humility that is the keynote of Husserl's early work from roughly 1900 to 1913.[5] For many late Victorians and Edwardians, man could no longer afford the luxury of believing he was unique. To play upon the title of an excellent study of Joyce's *Finnegans Wake*, the question had be-come not who is everybody when everybody is somebody else, but who is anybody when everybody is *something* else.[6] ALP and HCE become the River Liffey and the Phoenix Park not in the spirit of metaphor but in on-tological proportions, transferred easily from character to topography, and on to virtually any other structures of existence. A maneuver too preten-tious for some tastes, it is nonetheless the mark of much modernism and ought to be explained on the deepest cultural level.

Although Hardy often treats consciousness in a vaguely solipsistic way (the world hardly possessing any intrinsic meaning apart from the passions of the consciousness that views it), his greater talent searches within even the most impressionistic consciousness for modes of existence that are the same as those which characterize forests and animals and espe-cially fungus and fossils. This attitude allows the author to take as his sub-ject neither coal nor diamonds but the allotropic principle of carbon. This last metaphor comes from Lawrence's famous letter to Edward Garnett, in which he refuses to condemn even the Futurists because, although they limit themselves to finding the principles of physics in human character, they at least try to see such character in its participation with the non-human.[7] Hardy, as many critics have persuasively shown, habitually com-pares his characters with animals, plants, topography, weather, geology, not as though something in their character were merely like the natural thing or event but as though the allotropy were being sought, as though the same manner of being had been wrought in both by larger forces and processes.

Hardy speculated, for instance, that the "intention" of creation had been somehow "blighted" so that "the leaf was deformed, the curve was crippled, the taper was interrupted; the lichen ate the vigor of the stalk, and the ivy slowly strangled to death the promising sapling." So also in this same novel, *The Woodlanders*, Grace's character and situation are similarly blighted: "Acorns cracked under foot, and the burst husks of chestnuts lay exposing their auburn contents as if arranged by anxious sellers in a fruit market. In all this proud show some kernels were unsound as her own situation, and she wondered if there were one world in the universe where the fruit had no worm, and marriage no sorrow."[8] She sounds much like Tess, who also asks about blighted apples and worlds.

But this ontology of blightedness is not the sole or even the main link in Hardy's mind. In fact it is one of the more formal of such associations, having been suggested in part by Edward Von Hartmann's *Philosophy of the Unconscious* (translated into English and published in England in 1884). Far more often the allotropy arose very intuitively and spontaneously in his imagination, as with this material from the first draft of *Far From the Madding Crowd*. I quote here from Christine Winfield's discussion of the manuscript in connection with Hardy's habits of composition and their bearing on the *Mayor* manuscript:

> Of greater interest still is the fragmentary sentence on f. 106f, completion of which is indicated by suspension points and a brief note (simply a phrase from *Hamlet*) incorporating the idea to be expanded:
>
>> the presence, of the fiery mist was caused by the effect of the hot sun's ray upon the swamp that afternoon . . . "god kissing carrion" etc. its color, of course, by the reflection and refraction of the sun's rays +
>
> The addendum to this note (indicated at the end of the sentence by the mark +) appears on the verso of f. 106e, and consists of a partially constructed sentence comprising only those aspects of the description salient in the author's mind; namely, the unpleasing anthropomorphic features of the objects described—an element characteristic of Hardy's handling of natural scenery. Blanks are left for material as yet unformulated: "desc. these fungi thus. Then there was the ——— with its bloody skin and ——— spots. . . . There was also" (f. 106e). Immediately above this note further de-

tails of the fungi (written in pencil and later erased) have been added: "clammy tops, crowns, oozing gills—splotches red as arterial blood."[9]

As we shall see in discussing *Far From the Madding Crowd*, Hardy's memory of the phrase from *Hamlet* combines with far more than a taste for "unpleasing anthropomorphic features" to create a highly intuitive allotropic lead, one which he contrives to leave open for meditation until he can fill in the blanks not only with proper names for the fungi but with language worthy of the paradox in Shakespeare's original phrase. He has, in short, caught the scent and will almost literally pursue the quarry to earth. This phenomenological instinct in Hardy, then, *uses* the wispy subjectivism of a Fitzpiers or of a Tess thoroughly mesmerized by Angel Clare and seeks not only to mark these allotropic channels but to run in them itself.

Far from being an early chapter in the modern loss of self, however, Hardy offers thereby an expansion of self that he senses is necessary if identity is to survive at all, for either the novelist or the layman. He offers it not in the pseudoscientific language that D. H. Lawrence appropriates for the purpose, but, sensing that such expansion may well be something quite ancient, in the loose confines of the pastoral. The pastoral had always offered some sort of analogous expansion—however literary and symbolic that treatment of Nature may have been—through its ill-defined but catholic virtue of "otium," a quality similar to one that William Barrett finds at the heart of phenomenology.

Barrett has suggested that although phenomenology has become a highly complex discipline, its original impulse was toward a new humility of mind, a tranquil readiness that was content to let things reveal themselves before one began tailoring them to larger and ready-made conceptions.[10] One could search for a single word or quality to express this revolutionary attitude in art during the very beginning of the modern period. Certainly much of the era resists Kant's division of reality into *noumena* and *phenomena*. Schopenhauer declares his opposition to that dichotomizing and Husserl does too, although in most ways they are entirely different philosophers. Phenomenology arises from this rejection and suggests that if we trust the subjective impression with the humility Barrett suggests, it will—and only it can—dissolve this imaginary abyss between the phenomenal world and the realm of essences. The essence for a phenomenologist is already in the appearance, and the *fact* of the appearance—that such is the way it looks to me or feels to me—must, says Husserl early and late, be the basis for the necessary presuppositionless philosophy.

Barrett also argues that phenomenology proposes to return to some primordial sense of truth as *aletheia*, "unhiddenness":

> Truth happens when a thing comes forth from the hidden into the open, from the darkness into the light, and is revealed as what it is. And we ourselves are capable of truth to the degree that we can let the thing be what it is so that it can shine before us as it is, while the veil of abstractions—woven either by our routines or by other people's empty phrases—falls away. Then we see, as it were, for the first time. "I know" in ancient Greek is *oida*, literally "I have seen."[11]

My own view is that this is a large part of Joseph Conrad's implication in the Preface to *The Nigger of the Narcissus* when he says that above all he wants to make us "see," and that an equally large part of Conrad's impressionism is concerned with this sort of epiphany rather than with the relativistic "truth" of the impression only, the much-touted inability of the reader to pass beyond the various impressions made by Lord Jim upon assorted listeners and viewers. If this interpretation of Conrad's impressionism is valid, his method is far from relativistic and leads, on the contrary, to a phenomenological faith that the greatest variety of impressions among a variety of observers is the only way to improve our sense of the thing in itself, much as Husserl and Gaston Bachelard encourage a revery of subjective, poetic views of the same thing. At the very least there is in Conrad's impressionism the same paradox inherent in the larger Impressionistic movement itself: seeming in the end to encourage relativism, it nonetheless began in fervent attempts to return to the certainty of primordial perception.

In Hardy, it is only on the phenomenological level that one can see the nonhuman in the human, the sunlight in the depths of the hazel copse producing literally the same effect as the sun striking Elizabeth-Jane's loose hair, for example. And it is in this ambition to pass beyond the overweening rhetoric and philosophic rumination of his characteristic style that we find him moving from the sense of truth as *wahr* (connected with *be-*

wahren and *wary*, to guard and defend what we believe has permanence)[12] toward that willingness to strip away the old frames and lift the conceptual nets in favor not of defensively guarding what may be permanent but of surprising a thing being itself. The kind of ontological clue or lead that, once surprised, allows this expansion of the human into the nonhuman and of the psychological and moral into the ontological I shall demonstrate in *Far From the Madding Crowd*. It is the pastoral mood itself that encourages—as it anciently had—the elegant movement. If Conrad's apparently contradictory impressions of Lord Jim lead nevertheless to some unified sense of Jim's manner of being, in Hardy we proceed on the contrary not primarily from the impressions of one point of view to those of another and yet another but often with diminishing returns from one of the author's philosophic or rhetorical attempts to frame his creation to another—some of them offered to the reader fully and seriously deployed, others abandoned in mid-construction and presented almost as self-parody. These framing attempts constitute the most blatant and notorious aspect of Hardy's style, and it is, I believe, this aspect of Hardy which manipulates chance, creates grand theories of Universal Will, and bemoans our sheer victimage in an indifferent universe.

It is the other Hardy to whom I turn, the one who answers to the oaten strain, and that even when far from the sheepfolds. It is this Hardy who in being most ancient is most modern. This pastoral talent is not merely a peculiar twist given to certain images, but—to use Husserl's term—the "intention," the world as lived by his imagination; Hardy's use of the pastoral strongly influenced D. H. Lawrence and is the determining factor in modern conceptions of "character." The Victorian novel was much given to conceiving character in terms of society and social relations; even the characters of *Wuthering Heights* and Charlotte Brontë's notorious madwoman in the attic bear a remarkably complex social significance. Only with Hardy is the conception permanently expanded to include our affinity with forces and substance beyond even the collective human will. If we read Hardy with this new emphasis, he seems less the railer against fate and more the quiet student of these tenuous filaments that lead not only to other people but to the earth and nonhuman life itself. Occasionally in the midst of one of his cosmic protests or theories we can drop our eyes from the face of the performing public figure and watch his hands belie his performance, watch his fingers quietly trace some puzzling strand of clues as though he were one of his own rustics who knows that while the mind can betray, the touch is all.

I propose, then, to look at the development of the pastoral in *Far From the Madding Crowd, The Return of the Native, The Mayor of Casterbridge, The Woodlanders, Tess of the d'Urbervilles,* and *Jude the Obscure,* in order to watch Hardy discovering in its ancient sensitivities the very pulse of phenomenological modernism. In doing so we shall see not Hardy the tragedian or Hardy the cosmic pessimist nearly so much as a Hardy who attempts to reshape the pastoral's ancient virtue of "otium" for survival in a new Nature.

One
Far From the Madding Crowd

Critics of Hardy have never made clear that whatever other pastoral elements may be present, Gabriel Oak and Bathsheba of *Far From the Madding Crowd* represent a truly remarkable, indeed a virtuoso, set of variations on the old pastoral opposition of otium and the aspiring mind. Of course the pastoral lent a great many shades of meaning to both ideas. As Hallett Smith points out, the distinction suggested everything from Bacon's contrast of Abel and Cain as the contemplative shepherd and the active husbandman, to the Stoic avoidance of ambition. Smith argues persuasively that the "central meaning of pastoral is the rejection of the aspiring mind" and offers a number of Elizabethan examples, quoting Marlowe's Tamburlaine:

> Nature that fram'd us of foure Elements,
> Warring within our breasts for regiment,
> Doth teach us all to have aspyring minds.[1]

If the aspiring mind is variously epitomized by Pompey and Mary Queen of Scots, and is a direct contrast to "the attitude of the angels," surely we may add to Smith's Elizabethan list the Satan of Milton, whose sin is precisely to refuse his place in the great hierarchies of mind and universe. The aspiring mind will not see freedom, in the proper Miltonic sense, as obedience to the right authority, and it characteristically refuses to find its own essence in any "proper" relationship to a hierarchy. As with Milton's Satan, the aspiring mind invariably sees in hierarchies the possibility of an illegitimately imposed authority. While we must resist the temptation to call every less-than-contented mind aspiring, the mental self-sufficiency of otium nevertheless gives us the most useful contrast.

The opening two chapters of *Far From the Madding Crowd* represent a careful attempt by an ardent reader of Shakespeare's pastorals to complicate the fundamental opposition that had become traditional for most pastorals. We may set aside temporarily the obvious fact that Shakespeare's pastorals (and any of his characters "who doth ambition shun," to quote from *As You Like It*) lend Hardy's further peculiarities that might eventually be sorted out.² If for the moment we simply observe the delicate probing of Gabriel Oak's contentment in contrast to Bathsheba's almost contemporary feminism, it may tempt us to borrow Renato Poggioli's term "pastoral of the self" to describe what is going on. Somewhat in the way Marcela, in Cervantes' famous pastoral interlude in *Don Quixote*, seeks the pastoral life not for romantic love but for "freedom from love" and the "integrity of the person," so does Bathsheba appear to bear the burden of a sensibility that aspires to an identity achieved apart from conventional love and marriage.³

She is introduced to us with a quality essential to many versions of the aspiring mind; she is, as Oak observes, vain, whereas Oak himself is the model of cosmic humility: "And from a quiet modesty that would have become a vestal [an important allusion], which seemed continually to impress upon him that he had no great claim on the world's room, Oak walked unassumingly, and with a faintly perceptible bend, yet distinct from a bowing of the shoulders" (3).⁴ The care with which Hardy operates in these first two chapters is suggested both by the reference to "vestal" and by the distinction between a faintly bent body and a bowing of the shoulders. As many critics have observed, Oak's is not a passive acquiescence in nature's ways; he is neither intimidated nor particularly uninventive. If virginal, there is indeed an almost sacramental quality to his innocence; it is the innocence of one who perhaps knows much of what there is to know about the indifference of nature to men's aspirations and who yet has achieved a kind of contentment. Like the vestal virgin to her goddess, Oak means far more to Hardy than simply the quality of being uninitiated. On the contrary, it is his almost perfect and steadily increasing knowledge of man's relation to nature and "fate" that we value—and which Bathsheba will come to value above all things.

Oak is of course described from the outset in similes and metaphors of rustic nature. When he smiles, the wrinkles around his eyes extend "like the rays in a rudimentary sketch of the rising sun" (1). He remedies the defects of his broken watch by "constant comparisons with and observations of the sun and the stars" (2), as well as by staring unembarrassed into his neighbor's windows in search of a clockface. His watch is withdrawn from its pocket "like a bucket from a well" (2). Only a Gabriel Oak would seriously ponder the fact that there was no "necessity" for Bathsheba to peer into her small looking glass as he first observes her passing in the wagon, neither to "adjust her hat, or pat her hair, or press a dimple into shape" (5). He cannot grasp simple vanity.

Oak, furthermore, is a man of the median, Nicomachean in his very conception: his features "adhered throughout their form so exactly to the middle line between the beauty of St. John and the ugliness of Judas Iscariot, as represented in a window of the church he attended, that not a single lineament could be selected and called worthy either of distinction or notoriety" (6). Which is not to say that he is undistinguished. The description serves to place him firmly in that class of historical figures whose instinctive avoidance of extremities makes them, as Aristotle argued, the model of virtue: for virtue lies in determining or knowing almost instinctively the middle road, as do contentment and otium. Ambition speaks of extremes—and so we have this peculiar linking of contentment and virtue that may go back to Aristotle in the *Nicomachean Ethics* as much as it does to Stoicism or the earliest forms of the pastoral. The virtuous man does not pursue experience for its own sake (and thus go to extremities where the word *experience* is so generously used). Gabriel Oak is meant to be far more than the rather dull but dependable man whose great virtue is his staying power; such tenacity, after all, partly derives from his being very much in harmony with such aspects of nature as admit of it.

The first chapter ends as a reader of the pastoral might expect, with Oak pronouncing the name of Bathsheba's—as he sees it—great fault; and it is also the name of the quality most often associated by tradition with the aspiring mind: vanity. It is the last word in the chapter.

And yet it hardly describes Bathsheba. Hardy is no more satisfied with it than he would be with some rough-and-ready term for Oak's contentment. The idea of vanity is, however, given a subtle twist quite early in the following chapter when the narrator advises us that on a clear night, gazing up at the stars, "the roll of the world eastward is almost a palpable movement." Out on the hill at midnight, as Oak and pastoral folk often are, "having first expanded with a sense of the difference from the mass of civilized mankind," you may "long and quietly watch your progress through the stars" (9–10). This vividly described feeling is no doubt meant as some sort of counterpoint to Bathsheba's gazing in the hand mirror, turning inward with vanity while Oak and his pastoral brethren turn outward and upward to the stars and to what may be the most fundamental natural motion of all. Bathsheba, after all, tired of nursing a sick cow, is sufficiently aspiring and unpastoral to wish she were "rich enough to pay a man to do these things" (15), though Hardy is quick to reaffirm his own pastoral tone by saying, only a few lines after her declaration, "Between the sheep and the cows [giving birth] Lucina had been busy on Norcombe Hill lately" (15). Even the pastoral sense of the earth's motion through the stars, however, is subject to Hardy's characteristic appreciation of ego as the fount of all impressions, however basically cosmic and selfless they may seem: "After such a nocturnal reconnoitre [in which the earth's motion is sensed] it is hard to get back to earth, and to believe that the consciousness of such majestic speeding is derived from a tiny human frame" (10). But it *is* derived from a tiny human frame. Even in its most potentially selfless and cosmic and ennobling perceptions, the pastorally tuned mind must have its own kind of "vanity" and self. We are not simply to oppose Bathsheba's mirror and the earth's felt motion through the stars, her vanity and Oak's almost graceful, selfless consonance with nature. It is perhaps unnecessary to repeat what so many critics have said, that despite Oak's consonance with nature he is presented as a man who understands how to manage and manipulate nature's own blind forces rather than simply roll with them; even the notes of his flute are interestingly described as a "sequence which was to be found nowhere in nature" (10) and which brings something generically different to the hill.

If Oak's "special power, morally, physically, and mentally, was static, owing little or nothing to momentum as a rule" (11), Bathsheba's performance on the horse as Oak covertly watches is nothing short of ideal motion. In this well-known passage she passes under low boughs by dexterously dropping "backwards flat upon the pony's back, her head over its tail, her feet against its shoulders, and her eyes to the sky. The rapidity of her glide into this position was that of a kingfisher—its noiselessness that of a hawk." She rides a man's saddle, and "springing to her accustomed perpendicular like a bowed sapling, and satisfying herself that nobody was in sight, she seated herself in the manner demanded by the saddle, though hardly expected of the woman, and trotted off in the direction of Tewnell Mill."

All of these images associated with Bathsheba serve to do far more than suggest that her movements are *like* several in nature. Rather, both terms of the comparison suggest an allotropy of the sort D. H. Lawrence sought

(18). In contrast to the grace and near "genius" (15) of her motions and manner as she rides the horse and as she comes from milking the cow, Oak's face, watching her, is seen "rising like the moon behind the hedge" (19). Both the images surrounding this aspect of Bathsheba and those characteristically applied to Oak are, however, natural and allotropic. The difference, of course, is between the relatively static and dependable, on one hand, and the startlingly quick and supple on the other. In the case of Bathsheba's riding, however, we must also make the rather mundane observation that she is dangerously close to being, in Victorian eyes, unladylike. We are being introduced to an aspect of her character that explains why she is offended by Oak's announcement that he had seen her performance: "not by seeing what he could not help [seeing], but by letting her know that he had seen it" (21). More even than this, she is annoyed that "Gabriel's espial had made her an indecorous woman without her own connivance" (21). Presumably she is game for a certain amount of indecorousness that *is* of her connivance.

She is a woman who wants to control her variations from the Victorian norm as a declaration of identity, not suffer them from the mere accident of being seen. We have encountered something of her type before, surely in Jane Eyre and in some of George Eliot's heroines, but never I think with the ultimate resonance Hardy's pastoral form and contexts lend. Like Maggie Tulliver, she is "that novelty among women—one who finished a thought before beginning the sentence which was to convey it" (23), while Oak, as we expect, doubts his ability to convey any feeling in "the course meshes of language" (23). Oak is epitomized by his name, at peace with it, and rather pleased that it is the only one he will ever have. "My name is Gabriel Oak." "And mine isn't," she replies, achieving at once both the evasiveness she values and the introduction to a thought completed momentarily when she declares that her name sounds "odd and disagreeable," and Oak counters with as much wit and conventional flattery as he can muster: "I should think you might soon get a new one" (24).

No great prescience is needed to see that if Bathsheba is to get a new name it must be both ontologically revealing and one that she earns, not simply a married name. She is fiercely resistant to the traditional notion that a woman derives a large part of her identity from the man she marries. Bathsheba does not like her name, but she would never refer to herself as "somebody," as Oak does when he comes to propose marriage a short time later: "Will you tell Miss Everdene that somebody would be glad to speak to her" (29). Hardy attributes Oak's use of the term "somebody" to an admirably pastoral "refined modesty," but we are left to observe that Bathsheba's attitude toward names is nonetheless remarkably different. She runs after him later not really to encourage his suit but to refute her aunt's claim to Oak that she must already have a "dozen" admirers: "I *hate* to be thought men's property in that way, though possibly I shall be had some day" (32).

The precise quality of her independence is suggested delightfully by her notion that she "shouldn't mind being a bride at a wedding, if I could be one without having a husband. But since a woman can't show off in that way by herself, I shan't marry—at least yet." Jane Eyre feels, more than any other Victorian heroine before Hardy's, the need to establish her own identity (indeed, self-image) *before* yielding to the powerful defining qualities of Rochester and her passion for Rochester. She fears being absorbed by him, and, as is sometimes suggested, it is curious that one feels Rochester must somehow be tamed (or even maimed) before Jane can come to him, fully herself.

Bathsheba declares to Oak that she needs "somebody to tame me; I am too independent; and you would never be able to, I know" (34). But it is not really true that Bathsheba needs to be "tamed" by her involvement with Sergeant Troy and Boldwood before she can come to Oak. We do not have a dishonest novel here in which Hardy eventually abandoned the vision of a really independent woman in favor of some compromise between the independently realized self and the old, male-dominated ways. Bathsheba's half-comic vision of herself as a bride at a wedding without a husband is strangely anticipatory of Tess's baptizing her own baby. What Bathsheba really suggests is that there ought to be a publicly acknowledged way for a woman to "succeed" without simultaneously submerging herself in a husband's name, position, and sex. I am not speaking of a woman who does not need a man or cannot love or feel dependent. As everyone agrees, in encountering Hardy's women we are walking up-country, and ahead, ominous and inviting, lie the foothills of D. H. Lawrence. Between Charlotte Brontë's characters and those of Lawrence an even greater distance lies. Jane Eyre displaces her legitimate claims on herself for—to use Freudian logic—the substitutions of maniac wife, burning mansion, and maimed Rochester; Birkin and Ursula in *Women in Love* slug it out toward some healthy "star-equilibrium." In Charlotte Brontë we have an author who cannot (because of the prejudices of her audience) or will not (because of some internal, personal censorship) admit the real goal of Jane's life. Not only does Lawrence *know* what the woman's issue is, he is often in danger, as Ursula says of Birkin, of talking it to death. Hardy lies somewhere in between.

It is worth noting that chapter 4, "The Departure of Bathsheba—A Pastoral Tragedy," refers not to the departure of Bathsheba as tragedy but to Oak's loss of his sheep through the "tragic" excesses of the sheep dog known only as the son of George. The whole chapter verges on the mock-pastoral, almost as though Hardy had not quite decided what his own attitude toward the convention itself ought to be. Finally, however, all the half-humorous pastoral allusions coalesce in a pastiche of tragic action which, while the tone is light, is as close to real tragedy as Oak is ever likely to come. The point is, of course, that Oak ("placid and regular," "even-tempered") is as unlike Bathsheba and—not to make a joke—the son of George as we can imagine. The young dog, unlike his father, has "insuperable difficulty in distinguishing between doing a thing well enough and doing it too well" (38); his is a tragic personality, much given to extremes.

We laugh at this comic reduction of scale: the personality of dogs cannot be or not be tragic. Yet Hardy has led our attention not only to the question of the legitimacy of his half-comic tone (especially in view of what happens to the sheep) but to the whole idea once again of the middle way and the danger of extremities. Even young George's son, in short, is part of an ethical pastoral context far deeper than such gratuitous mock-heroic as: "He called again: the valleys and furthest hills resounded as when the sailors invoked the lost Hylas on the Mysian shore; but no sheep." Oak is carefully identified as the shepherd in feeling as well as trade, as in at least some rudimentary way analogous to the shepherd metaphors of the Bible and Milton: "A shadow in his life had always been that his flock ended in mutton—that a day came and found every shepherd an errant traitor to his defenseless sheep. His first feeling now was one of pity for the untimely fate of these gentle ewes and their unborn lambs" (41). Thus perhaps the Hylas simile is both mock-heroic and deeply felt: as the beautiful lost Hylas (captured by nymphs) is to Hercules, so *in proportion* are the lambs to Oak, no less beautiful, no less lost.

George's son is "tragically" shot, "another instance of the untoward fate which so often attends dogs and other philosophers who follow out a train of reasoning to its logical conclusion, and attempt perfectly consistent conduct in a world made up so largely of compromise" (42). While it may be a mistake to wax solemn about Hardy's humor, the tone of the whole chapter simply cannot be as light as the phrase "dogs and other philosophers" suggests, and we wonder whether Hardy really has the inflection under control. He never forgets for one moment that the level of these events is not Sophoclean, not even that of Hercules and Hylas; he is anxious to put all in perspective, to assure his audience that he knows this is just an untutored shepherd confronted by the double misfortune of loving a complex woman (moving fast out of his orbit) and losing the sheep by which he thought to rise modestly in the world.

Still, even that desire on Hardy's part does not explain or forgive something like the following: as Oak peeks into the cow shed where he sees Bathsheba for the second time, Hardy notes that he cannot see her very well, her position being almost beneath his eye, "so that he saw her in a bird's eye view, as Milton's Satan first saw paradise" (14). The disparity between Oak's view and Satan's, between Oak and Satan and Bathsheba and paradise, is so grotesque that one is tempted to believe either that a fairly young author is simply showing off (and not very successfully) or that in his attempt to produce a faint echo of mock-epic, mock-heroic tone, he has gone too far. In fact, what we must account for is Hardy's apparent feeling that the mock-heroic tone is required at all. Is it just that he knows his audience will be so embarrassed at anyone's taking shepherds and the habits of sheep dogs seriously that he must anticipate them with the inherent irony of using the language of epic and tragedy for rustic matters of this sort? I think the best explanation may be that Hardy was unable, at this early point in his career, to see how seriously the pastoral world was to figure into the ethical and psychological foundations of his work. And so he keeps it at an aesthetic distance by a rather awkwardly applied half-serious tone which was scarcely necessary in the entirely unpretentious *Under the Greenwood Tree*.

That tone is belied, however, by one of the few elements of chapter 5 that entirely escapes it, the famous image of the "oval pond" that Oak broods upon immediately after realizing what has happened to the sheep. Literary shepherds are prone to look to heaven, to the evening star, to nature in general, for confirmation of its healing and restorative powers, especially in the case of the pastoral hero who flees the "world" to find his soul in the pastoral otium. Here too nature speaks, but with an image that is as far from "Lycidas" or "The Garden" as it is possible to be and remain in the same broad literary tradition:

> By the outer margin of the pit was an oval pond, and over it hung the attenuated skeleton of a chrome-yellow moon, which had only a few days to last—the morning star dogging her on the left hand. The pool glittered like a dead man's eye, and as the world awoke a breeze blew, shaking and elongating the reflection of the moon without breaking it, and turning the image of the star to a phosphoric streak upon the water. All this Oak saw and remembered. (41)

Even without any detailed analysis of this powerful image, it is important that we recognize its place in a long tradition of shepherds who look to nature for meaning, indeed for a confirmation of their otium in the very scheme of things. In this late-Victorian instance, however, all is dissolution and exhaustion and loss. Images decay and even the image of that decay is "dogged" and blurred. More significant than these observations, however, is the simple note that Oak "saw and remembered." He now knows what the relation of man to nature is, and it is above all not the relation of shepherd to flock. Far from this destroying his pastoral identity, it seems to confirm for both Oak and Hardy the need for a new pastoral, one in which the old values are made to accommodate a new perception of the universe. We are at the *locus classicus* of a post-Darwinian pastoral that Hardy was to worry with an intensity surpassing even the son of George.

One of the consequences of Oak's losing his sheep is, ironically, that he must remain a shepherd. At hiring time no one seems to want a bailiff so Oak resumes the shepherd's crook and smock. Henceforth, he no longer pretends to the title *farmer*, and the word *shepherd* echoes with great significance through the early chapters. (Even as an incipient "farmer," however, Hardy refers to him as "pastoral king" [43].) Unable to find an employer at the fair, he draws out his flute and plays "with Arcadian sweetness" (45). He still sleeps well, "shepherds enjoying, in common with sailors, the privilege of being able to summon the god instead of having to wait for him" (47). In short, it is almost as though Hardy had contrived the loss of his sheep in order to keep Oak purely a shepherd. Having saved Bathsheba's ricks from total destruction with a strategic understanding of how drafts affect a fire, Oak confronts—much to his surprise—Bathsheba herself and asks with a thematic resonance: "Do you want a shepherd, madam?" She does indeed, "want" being understood in the sense of "need" more than of "desire." Her nearly tragic predicament will require all the old and "new" pastoral qualities inhering in this shepherd whom Hardy presumably grooms for the twentieth as well as the late-nineteenth century. "You are not a Weatherbury man?" asks Fanny Robin when Oak first encounters her on his arrival near Weatherbury. "I am not. I am the new shepherd—just arrived" (57). He concludes by insisting that he is "only a shepherd," but to my way of thinking he is, in the broadest context of Hardy's ambitious attempt to use the pastoral in the "new universe," truly the new shepherd, just arrived.

When Hardy contemplates the essence of rustics and rustic life, as he does with great intensity in chapters 8 and 9 in the ancient malthouse and the small "manorial hall" turned farmhouse which Bathsheba now occupies, he usually emphasizes the same harmonic: all the elements, whether architectural or human, are related to one another in an organic manner. There is an almost geological crusting and layering in the personalities, rooms, houses, names, malt-mugs, garden paths, and indeed in nearly every detail if Hardy sees fit to dwell on it at any length. Perhaps the key image is of the rustic folk as they are seen at dusk approaching Bathsheba's back door for their first interview with the new mistress: "A crooked file of men was approaching the back door. The whole string of trailing individuals advanced in the completest balance of intention, like the remarkable creatures known as Chain Salpae, which, distinctly organized in other respects, have one will common to a whole family" (86).

I suspect that this simile, which may seem to apply only to the common mission of seeing the new mistress for the first time, comes from a very deep intuition in Hardy, and that in fact the phrase "one will" has vast implications for his incredibly dense Darwinian background. The emphasis in the image is, after all, on individuals who retain their individuality in most respects and yet are bound together with a common will that does not appear to compromise that individuality. The conversations both at the malthouse and at Bathsheba's manor house are seemingly designed to affirm just this quality. It hardly need be said that one prominent form of the modern malaise (especially as it appeared to Hardy) was the deracinating isolation of the city man. Apparently, Hardy had even transcribed part of T. S. Eliot's *Prufrock* into his notebooks "before it became widely known."[5] In any case, the reaction of Bathsheba to Liddy's mildly humorous announcement that the "Philistines be upon us" is informative. She fully accepts the term that signifies a snobbish estrangement from this Chain Salpae approaching the back door (one is reminded of the Melstock Choir's visit to the new parson in *Under the Greenwood Tree*). Despite Hardy's marvelous care in delineating the strong individuality of each of these rustic visitors, one suspects that they are all of a piece to Bathsheba. We learn, however, that even the "stammering man" Andrew Randle, who cannot stutter two words in answering Bathsheba, lost his last job "because the only time he ever did speak plain he said his soul was his own, and other iniquities, to the squire" (89).

It is tempting to allow ourselves to be merely amused by this Shakespearian parade of rustics. Hardy does it vividly and even compellingly. Yet the morality of the scene cannot be discounted, especially as it concerns the tendency of Bathsheba to turn her back on the "common will" that connects these individuals. One may, with some justification, suppose that Hardy would gladly identify that common will with their function on the farm—or, more profoundly, in Nature. As they speak before Bathsheba, each identifies himself or herself in some fairly precise way with the great cycle of crops and seasons, planting and harvesting, and the birth and death of animals. Those "yielding women," Temperance and Soberness Miller, say they are to be identified by their "Tending threshing-machine, and wimbling hay-bonds, and saying 'Hoosh!' to the cocks and hens when they go upon your seeds, and planting Early Flourball and Thompson's Wonderfuls with a dibble" (87). Even the metrical rhythm of some of their answers suggests a connection with deeper natural rhythms.

We are surely not confronted here with noble savages or with some sort of ideal rustic innocence. Hardy is careful to introduce the vulgar, mundane, tedious, and just plain dull often enough to remind us that he knows whereof he speaks. He would like us to believe that he is not idealizing these people and their lives at all. At best, this is a delicate question for the student of Hardy. We can agree that he knows the real danger, discomfort, and even ugliness of the rustic life (though if Oak had followed his ancestors by sleeping outdoors or in a leaky hut, he would not have nearly suffocated). What is idealized, however, is the elusive quality of connectedness, or organicism. Henery Frey, unlike Bathsheba who dislikes and seems to seek distance from her name, insists on the extra *e* in Henery because it was "the name he was christened and the name he would stick to" (63). Cain Ball, misnamed by a mother who thought Abel killed Cain, is a constant stimulus to the memory of the community, not only of a mother "brought up by a very heathen father and mother, who never sent her to church or school" and thus allowed her to confuse Cain and Abel, but of the not entirely humorous fact that "the sins of the parents are visited upon the children, mem" (91). My point is that even the names of these people (which are so intimately involved in their identity) are densely inhabited, as it were—teeming with layers of the record of human dedication and fallibility. And both Henery and Cain in their own simple way live with this awareness, not only of their involvement with the past but of the danger of aspiring above such involvement (Cain would not think of and probably could not change his name). The naming of Cain Ball is not merely a historical fact that may have a certain amusing value when told to a sophisticated audience and a nearly "tragic" value when told to a sympathetic and rustic audience; it is, rather, an important part of Cain's present identity—not precisely the past but the past as lived in the present.

Once again it must be emphasized that the model for this connectedness is probably biological and evolutionary and not historical, just as Hardy's image of the approaching "Philistines" is drawn from biology and represents a rather delicate biological distinction. As a model it is also based upon the comparative and evolutionary method that informs even Hardy's description of Oak's astonished discovery that Bathsheba is the strange new mistress of the farm. Oak speaks in terms worthy of Edward Tylor or Frazer or another of the evolutionary anthropologists: "his Ashtoreth of strange report was only a modification of Venus the well-known and admired" (55). In the comparative method it is not that Ashtoreth historically antedates Astarte (or, probably, vice versa) and that both antedate Venus, but that all are forms of the one. In the comparative method the shift of perspective from culture to culture is often the equivalent of a movement backward or forward in terms of some sort of absolute history.

If anyone is expert in describing the truly "hoary" it is Thomas Hardy, whether his subject be the aged maltster, "his frosty white hair and beard overgrowing his gnarled figure like the grey moss and lichen upon a leafless apple-tree" (60), or the early Classic Renaissance house that Bathsheba now inhabits. In thinking about the organic relatedness that we have been discussing, Hardy was often given to architectural metaphors. As the moss, "like faded velveteen" (80), softens every angle of the building and seems about to reabsorb the structure into Nature, so the long life of the building has made its parts depend on one another as though living in one ancient body: "the stairs themselves continually [twisted] round like a person trying to look over his shoulder," and "Every window replied by a clang to the opening and shutting of every door, a tremble followed every bustling movement, and a creak accompanied a walker about the house, like a spirit, wherever he went" (81). The attitudes of Bathsheba and especially Sergeant Troy toward this building will become important later.

In pursuing Hardy's use of the pastoral, I am struck with the sense in which its most basic contrast of otium and the aspiring mind is reflected and refracted in a pervasive concern with the possible relationship between opposites. Part of Hardy's concern is no doubt inherent in choosing Oak and Bathsheba to begin with, but much of it seems to be a delicate probing of the precise nature of Oak's "middle way," and some of it is original philosophic thought of the highest order, fully realized as art. No doubt much of the novel is instinctively tuned to this phenomenology in a way that is more predictive of Lawrence in, for example, *Women in Love* (with its elaborate variations on the ancient mind-body problem) than the rather self-conscious dialectic of *Pride and Prejudice* or *Sense and Sensibility*.

The particular ontology we are talking about begins to make itself felt in chapter 11, in the amazing description of Fanny Robin's visit outside Sergeant Troy's barracks. In the description of the darkness and snow, all extremes are modulated: it was a night in which "love becomes solicitousness, hope sinks to misgiving, and faith to hope" (95). The persistent aesthetic exploration of the ways extremes may be related to one another is to blossom shortly into the subject of harmonies, most notably in the beautifully harmonious sheep barn and in the characteristically disjunctive psychology of Sergeant Troy. After all, harmony is itself the surprising resolution of qualities that tend toward disjunction, toward unresolved extremes. Harmony is a way of preserving not only differences but extremes in the very spirit of compatibility if not resolution; it is a state of existence which allows extremes and contrasts to retain their full flavor while bringing them into some sort of mutually illuminating relationship.

In Fanny's visit, however, extremes are not harmoniously related but annihilated. Following a marvelous description of the subtle stages by which winter advances on this peculiar section of meadow-moor, Hardy says that the climax had been reached this night, "and for the first time in the season its irregularities were forms without features; suggestive of anything, proclaiming nothing, and without more character than that of being the limit of something else—the lowest layer of a firmament of snow" (96). Even the snow-covered earth and the sky seem about to coalesce in an intimidating collapse of distinctions and differences and extremities, "for the instinctive thought was that the snow lining the heavens and that encrusting the earth would soon unite into one mass without any intervening stratum of air at all" (96). What Hardy envisions here is far more than a particularly depressing natural scene for the particularly depressing pathos of Fanny's relations with Troy (at least in this phase they are pathetic). It is in one of those remarkable passages that Hardy begins to assert the involvement of the nonhuman and the psychological in the same ontology, expanding our sense of human nature beyond personal and social relationships in a manner that was to be characteristic not only of D. H. Lawrence but of modernism in general.

The persistence of this collapse of distinctions throughout the scene amounts to a kind of phenomenological "white-out," if I may borrow a weather phrase familiar to polar explorers and residents of Rochester and Buffalo, New York. Confronted with one of these white-outs, in which one feels totally lost in a faceless, white sphere where earth and sky and directions may literally not be distinguished from one another, many a traveller has waxed philosophic. We may well wonder why Hardy associates its potent connotations with Fanny and Troy. One critic, wanting to contrast Fanny's relations with nature to Oak's, has noticed that Fanny is nearly always an anonymous "spot" or "blurred spot" in the landscape, in imminent danger of being simply absorbed, while Oak is always weather-wise and coming to grips with the problem of making nature work for man.[6]

But the reasons for associating this white-out with Fanny *and* Troy go far toward a phenomenology of harmony, both as it exists in Oak and the pastoral life and as it does not exist in Bathsheba and Troy. Troy, as his name would suggest, and despite the banality of his actual existence, is redolent of epic and military adventure; he has an apparently illegitimate drop of the nobility in him. In the medieval period that produced, as Hardy later notes, the ultimately harmonious sheep barn, Troy would have been associated with the castle, an institution which, like the church, simply cannot continue its medieval function into the present without great disharmonies resulting. The sheep barn, equally magnificent as these structures, can. The pastoral, somehow, can. Virgil's *Sixth Eclogue*, which is very much in Hardy's mind throughout this section (and, I suspect, throughout the novel) begins, after all, with the poet renouncing for the moment the epic and military strain ("When I was fain to sing of kings and battles") in favor of wooing "the rustic Muse on slender reed."[7] The history of the world next offered in the eclogue, full of terror as well as of pastoral harmonies, is the pastoral one of Silenus's songs and not the epic one of heroes and battles. The eclogue establishes at the outset the implication that Silenus's songs of the creation and history of the world are going to be in self-conscious contrast to another "history," the epic one. Even Fanny's visit is impregnated with this basic contrast between the disjunctions of Troy's "epic" psychology and the harmonies possible to a pastoral otium understood in an exceedingly delicate way.

In the snow-filled dusk of Fanny's visit, Hardy's description is reduced to vague intimations of shapes, "flatness," and "verticality." The neighboring clock striking ten is at first describable only as "an indescribable succession of dull blows, perplexing in their regularity, which sent their sound with difficulty through the fluffy atmosphere" (96). Although this may be only a good description of a particularly turgid night, I suspect Hardy is frightening himself in the manner of Joseph Conrad, whose characters often find themselves in fogs where all distinctions drop away to produce a primitive apprehension of the world laid naked. "A form" moves near the river; "By its outline upon the colorless background a close observer [and only a close one, presumably] might have seen that it was small [the most rudimentary of distinctions]. This was all that was positively discoverable, though it seemed human" (97). Even this mere "spot stopped, and dwindled smaller." The only hope for human identity in the scene is, apparently, to seem part of something larger: "This person was so much like a mere shade upon the earth, and the other speaker so much a part of the building, that one would have said the wall was holding a conversation with the snow" (98).

Here we are close not so much to surrealism as to a kind of naked ontology. This collapse of distinctions is the ontological opposite of harmony. It handles contrasts (such as sky and earth) in such a way as to annihilate them and is presumably a comment on the relationship between Fanny and

Troy as well as an anticipation by contrast of the burgeoning theme of harmony. Even the final laughter of Troy's comrades as they react to this soldierly tryst "was hardly distinguishable from the gurgle of the tiny whirlpools outside" (100). When we next see Troy, his symbol will be the "tangle" of his spur in the hem of Bathsheba's dress, which Troy wishes had been "the knot of knots, which there's no untying" (187). On some very deep phenomenological level the white-out and the profound tangle (which is no knot and never will be or can be so planned and conscious a thing as a knot) come to the same thing. In my mind both are forever in contrast with the elegant harmonies of the ancient sheep barn and with the harmony of past and present possible to certain states of mind.

Surely Hardy intends a sharp contrast with the movements of the nearly annihilated "blurred spot" when, in the next chapter, Bathsheba enters the Corn Exchange: "She moved between them as a chaise between carts, was heard after them as a romance after sermons, was felt among them like a breeze among furnaces" (102). Contrasts are not only restored to a healthy richness, but Bathsheba seems able to mediate them with natural skill, as the syntax itself now declares: "In arguing on prices she held to her own firmly, as was natural in a dealer, and reduced theirs persistently, as was inevitable in a woman. But there was an elasticity in her firmness which removed it from obstinacy, as there was a *naiveté* in her cheapening which saved it from meanness" (102–3). That she is no instance of Oak's "middle way" is, however, clear in the following chapter (I think the exact order of these chapters is important), when with "a small yawn upon her mouth" she addresses the valentine to Boldwood, an act which Hardy is anxious that we see in the context, again, of the possible relation between opposites.

Perhaps the key phrase for Boldwood is "the symmetry of his existence" (112). His life and very sanity are the result of great forces delicately balanced against each other:

> That stillness, which struck casual observers more than anything else in his character and habit, and seemed so precisely like the rest of inanition, may have been the perfect balance of enormous antagonistic forces—positives and negatives in fine adjustment. His equilibrium disturbed, he was in extremity at once. If an emotion possessed him at all, it ruled him. (137)

This is a good deal unlike Bathsheba's naturally modulated extremes in the Corn Exchange. What one does not yet know, however, is how intense and of what *conscious* power Bathsheba's talents in modulation may be. She is clearly unaware, as Hardy reminds us, that in a world where Boldwood's ontology is not uncommon, where outward rest is the result of enormous forces balanced against one another, small acts may have extraordinarily large consequences. In symbolic terms, the simple "marry me" red seal on the valentine burns itself into Boldwood's mind and seemingly becomes the red half-sun of the dawn following the valentine. Contemplating this sunrise, Hardy's mind once again meditates on the most profound implications of relations between opposites, saying that "the whole effect resembled a sunset as childhood resembles age" (114), a simile almost oriental in its labyrinthine faith that opposites depend on one another for their meaning and force. As Hardy describes the view in other directions at this moment, we find echoes of the white-out described in Fanny's visit: the snow has made it difficult to find the horizon, a "preternatural inversion" makes it nearly impossible to tell the sky from the earth, and we are once more threatened by the implosion of distinctions that are necessary for life and sanity. That this white-out should be associated both with Fanny and Troy and with Boldwood's growing obsession with Bathsheba is of course no accident. Yet we cannot say that it is simply *paysage moralisé* for the quality of blurring passion or blind love—it is far too deeply involved in other precisely ontological motifs to be so limited.

That Hardy's imagination is persistently visualizing intersections, contrasts, and possible relations between opposites, often in the most inventive way, is brilliantly demonstrated once again in the seemingly casual comment that the ancient maltster "seemed to approach the grave as a hyperbolic curve approaches a straight line—less directly as he got nearer, till it was doubtful if he would ever reach it at all" (117) and in the amusing inability of Joseph Poorgrass to remember which way *J*'s and *E*'s are supposed to face, "trying sons of witches" that they are (124). Fanny misses her wedding by going to All Soul's Church instead of All Saint's. Meaning to name her son Abel, a mother chooses Cain by mistake, and so on. Clearly what we are dealing with in this novel is a phenomenology which becomes a habit of mind affecting not only the broadest symbolic relationships but some of the most casual figures of speech.

Although human personality always involves opposites, one of the great structural elements of *Far From the Madding Crowd* involves a probing and demonstration of the contradictions in Bathsheba's character, followed by our immersion in the harmonies of the great sheep barn, followed almost immediately by the analysis of peculiarly violent disjunctions and disharmonies in the psychology of Troy. No doubt Hardy would have been at a loss to say rationally what the great barn has to do with the psychology of Troy. The author is working at a very intuitive pitch by this point in the novel; even to reduce his consonances and disjunctions to logical analysis seems cruel and damages the harmonics between psychology and landscape, between figures of language and the very structure of thought.

We are told, though we have seen it brilliantly acted out long before this, that "Bathsheba's was an impulsive nature under a deliberative aspect. An Elizabeth in brain and a Mary Stuart in spirit, she often performed actions of the greatest temerity with a manner of extreme discretion. Many of her thoughts were perfect syllogisms; unluckily they always remained thoughts. Only a few were irrational assumptions; but, unfortunately, they were the ones which most frequently grew into deeds" (149). Immediately following this description of the incongruity and disjunction of a mind whose form and content are seldom in harmony, Bathsheba finds Oak at the bottom of her garden "grinding his shears for the sheep-shearing": "The scurr of whetting spread into the sky from all parts of the village as from an armory previous to a campaign" (149). With this almost totally incongruous simile, Hardy induces us to think of other related oppositions: Oak and Troy, the pastoral and the heroic lives, otium and the aspiring mind (of which Mary Stuart had been a prime example to many Elizabethans), bucolic and epic, Oak's shearing and Troy's sword dance, and especially the general problem of how such opposites are to be important in this novel.

It is extremely significant, then, when Hardy concludes that "peace and war kiss each other at their hours of preparation—sickle, scythes, shears, and pruning-hooks ranking with swords, bayonets, and lances, in their common necessity for point and edge" (149). Although it is unseemly for Hardy to pursue the intention at this point, the anomaly of opposites "kissing" each other is to become an important addition to the deepest ontological perception of this fiction, a kind of yin and yang of the pastoral and heroic or active. It is not entirely humorous that Oak is described leaving Bathsheba (after quarreling and being dismissed), "as Moses left the presence of Pharoah" (154). Moses was one of the patriarchs who best illustrated the harmonies and self-possession of the pastoral carried over into the service of his people. Of course Oak is no Moses and Bathsheba is no

Pharoah (though she has been described earlier as a "thesmothete," or law giver, which I suppose would bring her even closer to Moses than to Pharoah). But then Oak calling his destroyed sheep is not the epic crew calling for a Hylas captured by nymphs either, though there is some question as to which is the more moving: a universe in which the divine may steal one away or a universe in which blind process and chance will deprive without caring. No doubt Hardy would rather lose the fairest Hylas to divinities who care enough about men to be impassioned by them. The tone that mediates between the elevated and the mundane (between Moses and Oak, Hylas and the dead sheep, say) is ambiguous in this novel. We are clearly not in the confident presence of mock-pastoral *or* mock-epic and must, I think, regard this as yet another dimension of the phenomenological inventiveness and playfulness in this meditation on opposites.

When Bathsheba's flock is swollen with wind from eating young clover, no one but Oak can perform the surgery; "Not even a shepherd can do it, as a rule" (157). If we simply ask what pastorals are most prominently in Hardy's mind in these introductory portions of the novel, the slight references to Moses, Milton's "Lycidas," and Virgil's *Sixth Eclogue* begin to fit together. Moses is almost archetypically the figure who has made the pastoral virtues cope with the most sophisticated complications and tragedies of the active world. He is the "good shepherd" who does not need to grow out of the pastoral virtues in order to lead his people; on the contrary, his pastoralism is the foundation of knowing how to care for his people in the upheavals of the exodus. That it is precisely this idea of the "good shepherd" which lies in the background of Hardy's mind here is confirmed not only by the quotation from "Lycidas" referring to sheep "Swoln with *wind* and the rank mist they drew [draw]" (156), but by the whole use of the incident with the young clover. Of all the things that might have gone wrong with Bathsheba's flock, Hardy's mind seems to have gone instinctively to the one that would allow him to use the quotation from "Lycidas" in conjunction with the main point of the episode: Bathsheba's helpless and feckless sheep are "such unfortunate animals!" in contrast with the enlightened, strategic, Moses-like expertness of Oak in transcending the ordinary notion of what shepherds can and cannot do.

Oak's facility in puncturing the sheep is important in revealing once again Hardy's insistence that this shepherd does not merely roll with the dumb forces of nature, but is a supremely strategic pragmatist. More than that, however, the quotation from "Lycidas" amply reminds us that the pastoral convention of the good shepherd is a way of talking about steward-ship and ethical responsibility, even spiritual well-being. Christ was the ul-timate good shepherd, and Milton's "swoln" sheep are misled by the "blind mouths" of false shepherds, leaders, preachers. In one sense, Oak is the good shepherd Bathsheba needs to see her though the Scylla and Charybdis of Boldwood and Troy. I should not like to make that process quite so pat and geometric as it seems. Any such claim for the relationship of Oak and Bathsheba makes it appear that Hardy is merely being ironic about her own aspirations toward becoming the good landowner, indeed the self-sufficient woman who will breakfast and be afield before her most diligent rustics. What is implied is a rather more complicated relationship between Bath-sheba's shepherding of her new land, flocks, people, and independence, and Oak's shepherding of Bathsheba. Both, it may be surmised, have a good deal to learn, though Bathsheba's drive to achieve an identity apart from any conferred on her by relationship with a man is treated very sympathetically by Hardy (always, however, with the reminder of a character known only as "Susan Tall's husband" wandering somewhere in the background, just to suggest comically that this identity problem may be reciprocal).

Although many critics have pointed to the importance of the great sheep-shearing barn, it has been difficult to relate its peculiar value to the larger questions raised in this novel, much less to its position between two rather talky but impressive descriptions of Bathsheba's and Troy's psychol-ogy. We should have no trouble, however, if two classic characteristics of the barn can be remembered and related to one another. First, the barn is continually likened to a church: "on ground-plan resembled a church with transepts. It not only emulated the form of the neighboring church of the parish, but vied with it in antiquity" (164). The magnificent chestnut roof "was far nobler in design, because more wealthy in material, than nine-tenths of those in our modern churches" (164).

Hardy is obliquely suggesting that in these late-Victorian times, when the church has become for him and those like him no longer a living con-nection with the past or a determinative spiritual experience, whatever the barn represents seems almost to supplant the church, to assume at least part of the church's former place in our consciousness. The great barn sur-vives as a spiritual experience when the church and castle cannot, because "the purpose which had dictated its original erection was the same with that to which it was still applied" (164–65). Unlike the church and the castle and superior to them, the barn represents a continuity of purpose and spirit from medieval to modern times. One takes from it a "satisfied sense of continuity throughout—a feeling almost of gratitude, and quite of pride, at the permanence of the idea which had heaped it up" (165). Hardy is extraordinarily pleased that although the purposes of the church and castle have been challenged, eroded, "worn-out," the barn allows "for once" medievalism and modernism to have "a common standpoint" (165). He concludes this first startling encomium to the barn by suggesting that the truth of all he has said lies in the permanence of our basic needs for food and clothing.

Of course the reasons for his enthusiasm and for the continuity of the barn are much less ordinary than that. What Hardy really seems to be saying is that the disjunction with the past which constitutes much of the modern *angst* can be obviated by finding the correct link rather than "worn-out" ones or ones that are positively misleading. In this passage we feel the delight not of the iconoclast who seeks disjunction but of the midwife who struggles to assist that new world "powerless to be born." It may be that for Hardy only a return to some spirit of the pastoral can provide the foundation for a new consciousness capable of discovering its own new harmonic with the past, not on the basis of religion or castle-and-crown history, surely, but keyed to the second great meaning of the barn.

Its continuity is due not so much to the fact that the sheep business has always been necessary to feed and clothe us, but that the barn is dedicated and conceived in a harmony that arises as one of the deepest needs of the human spirit. The barn's history is one of "functional continuity throughout," but the main point (as Hardy suggests by making this single sentence a paragraph unto itself) is that "the barn was natural to the shearers and the shearers were in harmony with the barn."

Thus the threshing-floor can compete with "the state-room floors of an Elizabethan mansion" not only in its patina but in the symbolic as well as economic importance of the ceremonies enacted there. Perhaps the most important symbolic dimension of this great structure is the functional simplicity of its architecture, form following function in a way that the architect Hardy would have profoundly understood. The lancet window openings combine "in their proportions the precise requirements both of beauty and ventilation" (164). We must not let the emotional intensity of this total description of the barn blind us to its logical consistency; the natural harmony of the barn with its function, and its people with both that function and the barn, is the key to the satisfying continuity between the medieval and the present. Just as Thoreau continually reminds his reader that he is not recommending we all trot off to the woods, so it seems necessary to remind readers of Hardy that no one is being advised to turn his back on "the madding crowd" in favor of a rustic and particularly a pastoral life. There is, however, the necessity to simplify radically one's perception of life in hopes of touching those wellsprings of human activity that lie even deeper than one's religion or politics or larger social and class orientation. The barn and not the church, however eloquent of the human spirit the church's architecture and history may be, is the link not only with the past, but more especially with the nonhuman world of Nature; the "spirit" Hardy would touch here lies beyond even the profundities of Christianity's two thousand years and takes us back to the ancient "Celtic" earthworks, to Stonehenge, and presumably to the earth itself in some chthonic appreciation of essential man as he blends with the modes of Nature's own existence.

That there is an essential man even beyond religious spirituality is one of the truly shocking implications of *Far From the Madding Crowd*, yet it is one of the main themes of D. H. Lawrence and of modern art. Usually the continuity of the barn has simply been attributed to Hardy's rather flip explanation that the need to feed and clothe ourselves goes beyond outworn creeds and the outworn social and military structures suggested by the castle. I think Hardy offers this cavalier explanation of his encomium to the barn partly out of fear of his position's fullest implications, for his argument here leads directly to Clym Yeobright and his return to Egdon Heath, if I may for a moment anticipate that subject.

It need hardly be said that Clym returns to the heath as a response to the ache of his modernism; Edgon is both his Walden Pond and his parched existential Atlas Mountains (after the manner of certain of Camus' stories). Clym flees the diamond business with its total involvement in the meaningless world of commerce and fashion not to retrieve any purely human spirituality, but so that he may once more feel those harmonies of ancient earthwork and earth, so that he may rediscover what lies in common between Nature and human existence. What is typically and beautifully Hardian about these links is that they lie even deeper than the most penetrating sense of the religious and spiritual life that he can muster, and

Hardy can elicit a good deal of that sense. Thus, he faces the religious crisis of the last half of the century by maintaining that the very terms of the disaster have been incorrectly formulated. It is no more exclusively a Christian crisis than is Clym's. To say that the old religion is dead or dying is, for Hardy, as well as for the newly burgeoning science or art of anthropology, to forget that it is not really a very old religion at all. Beneath the churches lie the Roman baths or cities or villas and beneath them the ancient earthworks and monoliths, the shapes themselves becoming more and more essential until we have what might be analogous to contemporary minimalist art: bare form, beyond even the massive simplicity of Stonehenge (which Hardy agonized at losing to commercial developers), and down finally to the flints of which one can hardly say whether they are man-made or natural.

It is no accident, however, that this nexus of ideas and feeling centering on the medieval sheep-shearing barn echoes with the word *harmony*. Our awareness of the past in the manner I have described makes at least two blessings possible if not likely. First, a new sense of beauty is born. Bathsheba's "loquacity that tells nothing" (167) tends constantly away from the awareness I have outlined, and Oak's "silence which says much" leads, albeit awkwardly for both character and author, toward it. The real immorality of at least some aspects of Bathsheba's "aspiring mind" is that they aspire away from the harmonies that permeate Oak and toward isolating ego, pride, and vanity. She cannot feel herself a part of something much larger than ego. The whole complex of associations centering on the barn gives birth, however, to what is both new and very ancient in the way of harmonious beauty. Gabriel's skillful shearing of the sheep gives us a new pastoral Aphrodite which we must not dismiss as merely an embarrassing display of Hardy's tendency to call in the Bible, Shakespeare, or the Greeks at the drop of a simile: "The clean, sleek creature arose from its fleece— how perfectly like Aphrodite rising from the foam should have been seen to be realized" (168). Bathos beyond compare, Cainy Ball now comes with the tar pot and stamps "B. E." upon the newly born Aphrodite! The new Aphrodite is nonetheless born of the swarm of feelings brought on by the pervasive harmonies of this barn scene. She is a true Aphrodite (as Hardy warns us), born of harmony as all beauty is.

The greatest consonance under consideration here lies potentially in the human mind. Oak has it, but in a way and with a quality that most readers will feel begs the question. Our best view of it comes from those other harmonies in the scene, between architecture and function, medieval and modern, shearers and their work and the barn, and from sensing that they are opposite to the psychological disjunctions of Bathsheba (who can be boldest with a manner of "extreme discretion") and especially of Sergeant Troy. What is needed also, beyond much doubt, contradicts Boldwood's mere "symmetry of . . . existence." Symmetry is not harmony, especially in the sense that Boldwood's symmetry is destroyed when he must live "outside his defenses." Harmony is not the implosion or merging or blurring of opposites (as in Fanny's visit to the barracks), nor—obviously— is it the "tangle" symbolic of Bathsheba's first meeting with Troy. At least in Hardy's insistence on moving from these subjective impressions toward purest eidetic patterns, *Far From the Madding Crowd* yields to a phenomenological analysis as do few novels.

The shearing feast, for all its undertones of discord, emphasizes an allusion to that lyrical harmony imposed by the old Silenus upon experience so diverse it has puzzled generations of classical scholars. After Bob Coggan's laughter has stopped Joseph Poorgrass's "poor plain ballet," "tranquility" is restored by Jacob Smallbury, "who volunteered a ballad as inclusive and interminable as that with which the worthy toper old Silenus amused on a similar occasion the swains Chronus and Mnasylus [Mnasyllos], and other jolly dogs of his day" (177). Of course Hardy knew the *Eclogues* in Latin while still a young man, and the earlier reference to the lost Hylas may well be explained by Hardy's remembering throughout this novel the *Sixth Eclogue*, which includes among its details "the tale of the spring where Hylas was left, and how the seamen called to him, till all the shore rang 'Hylas! Hylas!!'" (*Works*, 45). However Hylas got into the novel, Hardy invokes the reference as a contrast between two universes: in the one, as I have suggested earlier, divinity interferes constantly and with great interest in human affairs (the nymphs kidnap Hylas); in the other, blind chance in a godless universe (indeed the uncanny coordination of chance events) wrecks a man's fortune. The only plausible link between the diverse materials of the *Sixth Eclogue* is, as H. J. Lose has argued, that they are all in some sense stories about "how the gods interfered in human affairs for good or ill. Pyrrha (and Deukalion) cast the stones by direct command of the Earth-Goddess. In Kronos' days the gods dwelt among men, to their great advantage. Hylas was stolen away by water nymphs. Pasiphae was the victim of the anger of Poseidon or Aphrodite, the daughter of Proitos of the wrath of Hera."[8] And so on and on to account for every detail of the eclogue.

But of course the commonplace reputation of the eclogue is, as Hardy suggests, that Silenus's song is meant to be staggeringly inclusive and comprehensive. (The permutations of the "silenus" figure fill a book in themselves, including the idea of the "silenus" box, ugly outside but beautiful within.) The *Sixth Eclogue* begins with an Epicurean creation of the world, which consists mainly of the "forming together" of the four elements and continues with a mythological skipping around that, far from really seeking consistency as stories about the gods interfering in human affairs, flirts with one basic point: so entirely pleasing and disarming is Silenus's song that we will enjoy the most absurd pastiche of a universal history. This is a world song; all diverse elements of the narrative are reconciled in the pastoral delight of the manner in which the song is demanded and in the manner of its singing. If the opposites of fire, air, water, and earth can be reconciled for the sake of creating this world, who knows what diversity may be reconciled for the sake of creating Silenus's song!

Hardy's imagination, in quoting the *Sixth Eclogue*, has returned to one of his earliest visions of effortless harmony. His calling the song "interminable" is totally good natured. As the pastoral envelope of Silenus's song constitutes the very reason we delight in its almost silly diversity under the guise of comprehensiveness and universality, so the pastoral is beginning to function for Hardy as the key to a more obviously serious kind of world history and universality. Silenus's song is a talisman of Hardy's concern here with the harmony possible to the consciousness that he is describing by negation in Troy. After all, in a world which the gods have left, the echoing "Hylas! Hylas!" must strike in Hardy and in us an almost indescribable sense of loss. Hylas is only a most beautiful human; what *we* have lost is the divinity that took him. The "new Aphrodite" is to be found in man's consciousness, especially as it confronts the "new" and "modern" beauty of Egdon Heath in the next novel. It is noteworthy, however, that the shearing feast ends with the shattering of the delicate balance of extremes in Boldwood and with Bathsheba, "awestruck at her past temerity," going to another extreme in order to correct the first: "I have every reason to hope that at the end of five or six weeks . . . I shall be able to promise to be your wife" (180). Hardy's analysis of this final moment in the chapter is entirely in terms of disjunction and disproportion.

If it is true, as many critics allege, that Sergeant Troy is a character out of some ballad, a "blade" shameless in his flattery, living for the moment, and faithless to all but his own taste for variety, it is also true that Troy is a study in psychological disjunction that might be called characteristically modern. Following the brilliantly visualized "tangle" of their meeting, Troy is described in some of the novel's most objectionably abstract and verbose passages. Yet the emphasis throughout is that Troy, so verbally adept that he is rumored to have "learnt all languages" in school and to have gotten on "so far that he could take down Chinese in shorthand" (188), is a man unable to relate the various traditional parts and functions of the mind to one another. He is unable to project his consciousness into the past or future, and considering the importance of that function to Hardy this inability is saying far more than that Troy lives only for the moment, as blades are supposed to do. Oak, it will be remembered, despairs at ever being able to catch his meaning in the loose net of language; Troy can "take down Chinese in shorthand" but regards language not as a means of connecting various functions of the mind but almost of furthering their disjunction. He is precisely incapable of those harmonies of form and function, intention and execution, intellection and will, that allow the past to be part of consciousness. He is a cripple where normal processes of "expectation" (190), of projection into the future, are concerned. Moreover, "His reason and his propensities had seldom any reciprocating influence, having separated by mutual consent long ago. . . . He had a quick comprehension and considerable force of character: but, being without the power to combine them, the comprehension became engaged with trivialities whilst waiting for the will to direct it, and the force wasted itself in useless grooves through unheeding the comprehension" (191–92). Speaking "fluently and unceasingly," "he could in this way be one thing and seem another; for instance, he could speak of love and think of dinner; call on the husband to look at the wife; be eager to pay and intend to owe" (192).

In short, his inability to relate these various functions of the mind to one another has been topped by an ability, indeed facility, at letting them run in different directions at the same time. In Troy's potentially powerful but totally ineffective "force of character" and "will," the impairment is due, Hardy alleges, solely to his "being without the power to combine" comprehension and will. The fault is not with the power of either but with the talent for combining, relating them to one another. Coming to Troy as we do, after the great barn with its emphasis on consonance, relation, harmony, and proportion, we may agree that Hardy has created Troy as its obverse. The barn simplifies, and puts us in mind of Thoreau's admonition; Troy on the contrary is compulsively interested in and involved with "trivialities." His is totally a failure of *relation*, and in some respects comes close to the late-nineteenth-century portrait of the "paralyzed will" so familiar to readers of Conrad's early novels. In these Conradian portraits the mind "comprehends" what is right but is unable to will it. In the work of Flaubert, Huysmans, and Baudelaire, and in the delicate relationships between these literary uses and the philosophy of Schopenhauer, the paralyzed will came to be seen as a kind of *mal du siècle*. In Troy and in these other exotically flavored instances of the paralyzed will, the problem seems to be characteristically "modern," due in large part to something in the "new" universe.

Troy does not simply step out of an old ballad. He is a thoroughly deracinated young man whose only method of putting it all together (to use a definitively contemporary cliché) is in the elegantly controlled sexual violence of the sword exercise, where life and death, creation and destruction, emotion and the "carved" space of sculpture are all brilliantly related to one another. The exercise is symbolic precisely in the sense that it is a stunning counterfeit of all the delicately tuned proportions, relations, and harmonies his life so conspicuously lacks. It is one of the supreme ironies of the novel. Here he has all the control he ordinarily lacks; here the opposites are brilliantly related in a blurring symmetry of movement, "with just enough rule to regulate instinct and yet not to fetter it" (210). If we take instinct and rule to be yet another of the crucial dichotomies that this novel contemplates, surely Hardy has given us no reason to believe that Sergeant Troy can manage that relationship elsewhere in his life. In Sigmund Freud's collection of archaeological artifacts there was a Roman bronze head with the face of Minerva, suggesting reason and wisdom, on one side and that of a silenus full of impulse and sexuality on the other.[9] Freud probably valued the piece not only because it aptly illustrated the dual nature of man but because, containing both faces in the same small bronze and with a continuity of form, it suggested the dependence of one on the other and even the real possibility of a radical redefinition of both instinct and reason. So in Hardy's novel the meanings of opposites often modify each other in a most surprising way. Not in Troy, however. His opposites are severed, except in the sword exercise, which consequently has beneath the exciting sexuality and controlled violence of its surface a pathetic aspect.

This notion of the fatality and genuine decadence of severing relations between opposites was to mature in D. H. Lawrence until it became something of a definition of man, who is by nature a continuing struggle between opposites. Thus the African statues in *Women in Love* are the product of a culture which had severed the connection between mind and body long ago and had begun the long dissolution toward pure sensuality and instinct. What is necessary for Lawrence is the "star-equilibrium" achieved not only between two people but in the individual between the apparently opposing tendencies that nevertheless define his nature and each other.

This "newness" of Troy is again emphasized when Oak first sees him installed in Bathsheba's old manor house. He greets Oak from the window and remarks, "A rambling, gloomy house this" (271). To Gabriel's reply that it is nonetheless "a nice old house," Troy responds that he feels like "new wine in an old bottle here. My notion is that sash-windows should be put throughout, and these old wainscoted walls brightened up a bit; or the oak cleared quite away [!], and the walls papered." If we forget that Troy is an early step in Hardy's life-long attempt to portray the modern, the character of Clym Yeobright in Hardy's next important novel will be far more difficult to understand, as will the manuscript revisions which transformed Clym from a barely removed native to one who had felt the world's most "advanced" thought in Paris. Here Troy's newness is precisely destructive of the sense of harmony and continuity Hardy had earlier conveyed in the old place.

To clear the oak quite away would suggest far more, of course, than pulling out the ancient woodwork and wainscoting and perhaps sending Oak himself away. Hardy is not content to expose this aspect of Troy's newness but must have him continue to theorize about the relations of new and old in a comment that says much about Hardy's own method of creation.

A philosopher once said in my hearing that the old builders, who worked when art was a living thing, had no respect for the work of builders who went before them, but pulled down and altered as they thought fit; and why shouldn't we? "Creation and preservation don't do well together," says he, "and a million of antiquarians can't invent a style." My mind exactly. I am for making this place more modern, that we may be cheerful whilst we can. [271]

One not entirely facetious measure of how well Hardy made preservation and creation go together is the ease and delight with which the "new woman," Julie Christie, slipped into the movie role of Bathsheba. We may discover more substantial evidence that Hardy basically disagrees with Troy and the "philosopher" in his self-conscious preservation of the pastoral in this novel, a conservation which relentlessly extends that ancient form into the problem of maintaining old values in the modern world.

"Creation and preservation" is really a key phrase in any discussion of Hardy's use of the past. There is a good deal in the philosopher's comment that Hardy can agree with, and the truth of which he saw confirmed hundreds of times in his restoration of ancient churches. Style, as he had good reason to know, is very often based on a rather blind preoccupation with one's own time and place. There is no evidence that the Jacobean architect, had it been possible, would have preserved the Gothic, or that he should have at the expense of fully expressing himself. In the mouth of someone who was a builder himself, Troy's words would not sound so empty. But Troy has no capacity for relating the parts of his own consciousness and personality, much less the styles of different centuries, and so he is intuitively forced into a philosophic rejection of any style that would be based on relation and vitally include the past. Troy cannot know what Hardy takes as the harmonic of all his work, that the past is in the present even when we self-consciously exclude it: where is the past if we tear out a Gothic wall and replace it with a Jacobean design that is based on the discoveries of the Gothic arch? Has the past gone, or have we really destroyed the past if Steinbeck's proletarian grape pickers breathe the air that Virgil's Silenus breathed? Hardy does not say the past influences the present; it is *in* the present in an evolutionary way that Hardy learned deeply and permanently as young man.

If Troy's very name suggests the epic in contrast to the pastoral (and thus a hostile, intrusive element), it also suggests one of the most ancient civilizations and of course the very man, Schliemann, who saw no inconsistency in using the "fiction" of the past as a net of the clues to the present location of Troy. For the nineteenth century, Schliemann was the very personification of the relevance of past to present in a way that even the man in the street could understand, and he began excavating for Troy (in 1870) at almost the very moment Hardy began writing novels, just four years before the publication of *Far From the Madding Crowd.* The pastoral conserves and remembers though it often seems timeless.

Sergeant Troy, on the contrary, is in some bathetic ways suggestive of the psychology of the epic hero who is founder rather than continuer (though the irony is obvious, with impotent Troy quoting builders on the subject of how impossible it is to create and preserve at the same time). It is possible that correctly or not, Hardy saw in the psychology of the epic hero (especially Achilles) some of the disjunction and deracination he puts into the character of Troy, however absurdly wide the gap between them, and that in the ancient, pastoral virtue of otium he saw just the contrary quality of harmonic relation between the parts and functions of consciousness, leading to extraordinary continuities in time rather than the disjunction of a style that must destroy in order to create.

These are all very complicated and possibly subliminal matters for Hardy, but can we doubt that the association of that potent name *Troy* with these questions of past and present, creation and destruction, was somewhere churning in Hardy's mind? It is ironically the destruction of Troy that has preserved Troy for us in *The Iliad,* and for someone writing shortly after the actual rediscovery of Troy, the rediscovery would have seemed a conspicuously unexpected intersection of modern archaeology with ancient epic, of science and rationality with intuition and myth. The process of literary creation is incredibly elusive, but even these few guesses as to the meaning of Sergeant Troy deny his notion that creation and preservation do not do well together. They do very well together—almost as well as a silenus and Minerva in the same head.

The chapter called "Wealth in Jeopardy—The Revel" (36) begins with an image of nature which is so nearly reflective of Troy's mind that it serves to remind us how unnatural these contrary motions and disjunctions are:

> The night had a sinister aspect. A heated breeze from the south slowly fanned the summits of lofty objects, and in the sky dashes of buoyant clouds were sailing in a course at right angles to that of another stratum, neither of them in the direction of the breeze below. (274)

The sky itself seems to run off at odd, opposing angles, and indeed all of nature is full of signs that its customary harmony is about to fall apart not simply because a particularly violent storm is on the way but because the mental counterpart of this chaotic sky has assumed a position of authority at the head of the revel and in the life of Bathsheba. We have been prepared to see that the exposure of Troy's newness (or at least his taste for what he conceives to be new) immediately preceding the revel has a great deal to do with the peculiar lack of relation in his mind.

Thus two great Hardian motifs are related: the uses of the past and the pastoral psychology. Most readers have gone on to note how Troy violates what is natural to the rustics: brandy-and-water dangerously replaces the usual cider and ale, ignorance of the natural signs supplants the usual sensitivity (preserved, of course, by Oak) to messages from "Great Mother." Even the sheep respond to the impending chaos with a symmetry and purposefulness of design that stands ontologically contrary to the clouds running off in all directions and to Troy's seminal mental disjunctions:

> They were all grouped in such a way that their tails, without a single exception, were toward that half of the horizon from which the storm threatened. There was an inner circle closely huddled, and outside these they radiated wider apart, the pattern formed by the flock as a whole not being unlike a vandyked collar, to which the clump of furze-bushes stood in the position of a wearer's neck. (278)

I apologize for quoting so many of these passages in full, but part of my point is that in dealing with these very basic ontological differences Hardy is invoking the most intuitive levels of our awareness and suggesting (as T. R. Southerington has so nicely argued)[10] a great organism of man and nature, where psychology and natural phenomena are not merely related in *paysage moralisé* but as cosmic sympathies, as one part of a body reacts when another is sick. All this is very advanced Darwinism as much as it is poetic strategy.

We must notice, however, that not even Nature, Great Mother, can put signs into so pregnant a relation as Oak. Oak realizes that "two distinct translations attached to these dumb expressions. The creeping things seemed to know all about the later rain, but little of the interpolated thunder-storm; whilst the sheep knew all about the thunder-storm and nothing of the later rain" (27). If we are talking about the power of relating things to one another, this is an important paragraph. Great Mother herself is not so potent as human consciousness properly tuned. We are not to take whatever ultimate harmonies are possible to the mind (far beyond Oak's) from the beneficent influence of Nature, which simply does not have what we need. The pastoral is not primarily valuable for bringing man close to Nature for its calming and harmonizing influence. Nevertheless, only man can press these rustics back beyond the pastoral to the prehistoric life of caves and blind indulgence: the water-jug overturned amid the ruin of the now burnt-out revel "fell into the neck of the unconscious Mark Clark, in a steady monotonous drip, like the dripping of a stalactite in a cave" (280).

While ordinarily in Hardy some human quality or action will be compared with something in Nature, the gathering storm is likened to man-made fictions and affairs and art: "A hot breeze, as if breathed from the parted lips of some dragon about to swallow the globe"; "So unnaturally did it [a 'misshapen' cloud] rise that one could fancy it to be lifted by machinery from below"; "Time went on, and the moon vanished not to reappear. It was the farewell of the ambassador previous to war"; "A poplar in the immediate foreground was like an ink stroke on burnished tin" (281–84). Nature has become so unnatural that it must be compared with the affairs of men, whose capacity for the unnatural outdoes even the Great Mother.

Lest we forget that Bathsheba's original aspiration to uniquely feminine self-possession is part of Hardy's total use of the pastoral, he slowly allows Bathsheba to recapture her original self-image. We cannot, of course, believe her claim that only in a "turmoil of anxiety for her lover" had she "agreed" to marry him, but her further thought that "the perception that had accompanied her happiest hours on this account [of her marriage] was rather that of self-sacrifice than of promotion and honor" seems entirely accurate. "Diana was the goddess whom Bathsheba instinctively adored" (315). She longs for the "simplicity of a maiden existence" as against becoming "the humbler half of an indifferent matrimonial whole," and she longs to stand once more as she "had stood on the hill at Norcombe, and dare Troy or any other man to pollute a hair of her head by his interference!" (315–16).

This is not to say that her infatuation with Troy and even love for him is accidental. Like Artemis or Diana, Bathsheba is far from treating as an Actaeon every man who admires her. Even the legend is very complex about Diana's motives for maintaining chastity. The prohibition apparently extends to both male and female lovers; even her companion, the nymph Callisto, whom Zeus, disguised as Artemis herself, had tried to seduce, is killed. In originally begging her father for a tunic and bow and arrows rather than jewels or ornaments, she is reminiscent of Marcela in the "pastoral of self" during *Don Quixote*, demanding the right to be free rather than slip into the conventional role even the society of the gods has prepared for her. As Poggioli says in discussing Marcela's transformation of honor, chastity, and purity into something new: "For her, honor is no longer a social tie controlling moral conduct from outside, but an inner power ruled by no other law than itself. Chastity and purity are not the exterior signs of the ethical will, but spiritual manifestations of the integrity of the person."[11]

There is some reason to believe that Hardy associated Bathsheba with Diana and Artemis not as the fatal and vindictive goddess (even her priest in the grove of Nemi must be murdered to be replaced) and not as a man-hater surely, but as the fiercely independent being who would find her "integrity of the person" as the highest good, beyond the demands of sexual roles. Of course it is not inconsistent of Bathsheba to love Troy and even to fawn on him and play an outwardly traditionally feminine role to his exaggerated masculinity. That is not inconsistent with the integrity of self unless the attempt at this integrity is constantly threatened (as it is in Artemis and Marcela, usually by men or male gods controlled by a mythology of masculine behavior). As Samuel Richardson's Clarissa struggles for this same integrity, and is continually threatened by another man totally possessed by a mythology of supermasculine behavior, she is never more delicately feminine or capable of love. We may at this point begin to suspect that the continual aesthetic meditation on the possible relations between opposites in this novel (a focus which is really its phenomenological essence) culminates not even in the dichotomy of otium/aspiring mind, or pastoral/epic, or harmony/disjunction, but in the Lawrencian problem of how man and woman are to love and yet retain that integrity of self which worries Birkin in *Women in Love* so much and which is so conspicuously absent in the relations between Gerald and Gudrun. As in Lawrence the inner sanctity, and star-equilibrium between people, is always related to the internal question of maintaining connections between the opposing qualities of mind and body, so in Hardy the possibility of Bathsheba's achieving her integrity of the person while loving someone (and not constantly moving and fending people off as Diana does) is somehow tied in with her coming to terms with Oak's balance and self-possession. Hardy does not despise the peculiar nature of her aspiring (as the aspiring mind was disdained in the traditional Elizabethan pastoral) but rather admires it. He sees as Cervantes and Richardson did that many of the distortions of masculine life are due to men's refusal to allow women this integrity, and that if we would save ourselves we must, in a sense, convince Diana that she can stop running, put down her bow and quiver, release the hounds, and still be "free" somewhat in D. H. Lawrence's sense.

The beauty of Hardy's use of the otium/aspiring mind ambience is that in *Far From the Madding Crowd* he shows us how, with Bathsheba's particularly bold and ambitious aspiration, otium—far from being aspiration's genuine opposite and destruction—can be its salvation and fulfillment. This demonstration is a marvelous twist on the ancient opposition and suggests, I think, why in the presence of Fanny Robin, alive or dead, the ordinary contrasts of Nature always collapse and merge in some ominous blur. She is not even remotely a potential Diana, and the truth of the matter is that Hardy both as a novelist and as a man had little patience with women who were not—even if their potential were somehow perverted into a really frightening "integrity" (consider Sue Bridehead in this light). Even as Fanny's dead body is brought home for burial by the tippling Joseph Poorgrass, the first of the autumn fogs move in: "The air was as an eye suddenly struck blind. The waggon and its load rolled no longer on the horizontal division between clearness and opacity, but were imbedded in an elastic body of a monotonous pallor throughout" (323–24). Perhaps the phrase "sudden overgrowth of atmospheric fungi" (323) suggests even more vividly Hardy's profound emotional reaction to this simple girl who in the whole novel seems able to enlist the aid of only one large dog and Gabriel Oak. It is probably Troy's allegiance to Fanny even in death that wrenches Bathsheba back to her prior dignity and moves us rapidly toward the end of the novel. Like Tipsy Coggan, "one or the other of his eyes occasionally opening and closing of its own accord, as if it were not a member, but a dozy individual with a distinct personality" (329), the reader by this time sees "two of every sort, as if I were in some holy man living in the time of King Noah and entering into the ark" (330). Even in small amusing details Hardy is meditating on "two of every sort," and yet Fanny always inspires him to collapse these "twos," as she herself might have collapsed into Troy. She frightens Hardy more than Bathsheba at her fiercest, more even than Sue Bridehead. She inspires in him those ontological fogs in which Joseph Conrad's skippers apprehended the loss of all distinctions and the undifferentiated darkness behind all appearance.

After Bathsheba flees both the house and Troy's declaration of love for the dead Fanny, she spends the night outdoors and awakens within view of a small swamp that seems to her "malignant."

> From its moist and poisonous coat seemed to be exhaled the essences of evil things in the earth, and in the waters under the earth. The fungi grew in all manner of positions from rotting leaves and tree stumps, some exhibiting to her listless gaze their clammy tops, others their oozing gills. Some were marked with great splotches, red as arterial blood, others were saffron yellow, and others tall and attenuated, with stems like macaroni. Some were leathery and of richest browns. The hollow seemed a nursery of pestilences small and great, in the immediate neighborhood of comfort and health, and Bathsheba arose with a tremor at the thought of having passed the night on the brink of so dismal a place. (348)

This swamp is of course suggestive of the reaction that Bathsheba might have had to the revelations of the previous night (including the dead baby of Fanny and Troy). It is reminiscent of the sick brooding that possessed Boldwood. But it is significant that her most immediate reaction is shock at having spent the night "on the brink of" so awful a place. In a few moments Liddy appears and, not hearing Bathsheba's warning, steps lightly across the swamp, saying, "It will bear me up, I think" (349). The image of Liddy's doing so, "iridescent bubbles of dank subterranean breath" rising about her feet as she crosses, is unforgettably encouraging and symbolic to Bathsheba. She will recover, but not in any random way. The fungus image has appeared nowhere else in the novel with the impact it has here and as the fog covers the transportation of Fanny's body. And the image connected with dead Fanny is, as I have shown, also ontologically associated with the description of her visit to Troy at the barracks. Clearly the swamp image at Bathsheba's awakening is in some respects the culmination of that blurring and collapsing of contrasts which has haunted Hardy throughout the novel. Things fall and decay into the swamp and are reduced there to the grotesque colors and shapes of the fungi and, ultimately, to the bubbles of swamp gas rising about Liddy's feet and bursting, "expanded away to join the vapoury firmament above" (349).

Bathsheba will not join this sublimely obscene decay, reduction, and disappearance. The whole experience inspires her to stand her ground and reminds her of the sword exercise. She says to Liddy: "If you ever marry—God forbid that you ever should—you'll find yourself in a fearful situation; but mind this, don't you flinch. Stand your ground and be cut to pieces. That's what I'm going to do." She refuses to run away from her husband and *returns home*. The new Diana has been born. Offered the traditional consolations for women and wives who must be patient—to fill in the "carnations and peacocks" on her sampler and then to frame it and hang it beside her aunt's—she asks instead for some of her uncle's old books, a resilient and even comic list consisting of "Beaumont and Fletcher's *Maid's Tragedy*; and the *Mourning Bride*; and—let me see— *Night Thoughts* and the *Vanity of Human Wishes*" (352). Finally she refuses even these "dismal books" and asks for some romances and "*Doctor Syntax*, and some volumes of the Spectator," those monuments to mental equilibrium and awareness. She refuses tragedy, particularly Liddy's offer of the exaggerated masculine pride of "the black man, who murdered his wife Desdemona."

We do not, at the end of *Far From the Madding Crowd*, have a formerly independent and boldly aspiring woman who has been tamed by her experiences with Troy and Boldwood and especially by Boldwood's murder of Troy. Bathsheba finally seems to many readers a woman still young and now thoroughly dependent upon the solid and rapidly prospering Gabriel Oak. Yet it must be to Hardy's credit that the behavior leading to her marriage and the activating, as it were, of Boldwood contains precisely those disjunctions between motive and manner that the long, steady influence of Oak and of course her suffering with Troy and Boldwood can resolve. Bathsheba's aspiration toward an identity apart from the traditional role of women in her society is never treated by Hardy as another aberration to be smoothed out by Oak's pastoral harmonies or by the tragedies her behavior precipitates. Whatever we may decide about the reasons for Bathsheba's sending the valentine, constantly temporizing with Boldwood's mania, and falling adolescently in love with Troy, those reasons will not diminish my sense that at the novel's end her best basic vitality and identity as the new Diana are intact: in outgrowing those faults she has not been required by the author to sacrifice her feminism to some kind of general moderation and hard-won caution. On the contrary, the relationship between Oak and Bathsheba at the end of the novel is in some ways a more satisfactory vision of star-equilibrium between lovers than D. H. Lawrence himself could usually manage. Whereas Lawrence treats us to a vividly realized but finally confusing "Mino" chapter in *Women in Love*, in which he wrestles with the problem of how a woman can in some sense be dominated by a man and yet free, Hardy manages quite effortlessly to give us the final impression that even a subdued Bathsheba who no longer rides the fields giving orders (and who carries the full weight of her tragedies) is both committed to the moral authority of Oak and yet still a very independent spirit.

Perhaps in discovering his new Diana, Hardy intuitively retained something of her old reputation as a man-killer. She does, after all, leave two bodies on the way to Oak. But the only real death force in this novel is associated by Hardy with the annihilating white-outs, fogs, and fungus that suggest a collapse of all relation between opposites. A sensual dialectic of mind and body is precisely what Lawrence is offering, both in the wordy, often pedantic language of Birkin and in the sometimes comic bathos of Ursula. Hardy's inspired revisions of the old pastoral dichotomy of otium and the aspiring mind are, however, more flexibly ontological; they suggest not only the antidote to Troy's mind and Boldwood's monolithic obsession, but a way of imagining character that departs radically from the main stream of the Victorian novel. Unlike, say, Maggie Tulliver, who is defined largely in terms of her relation to the complex web of human society, Hardy's characters in this novel are rendered in modes of existence much larger than human relations and the society they produce. In his use of the ancient pastoral, Hardy is able to see man's participation in precisely the "non-human" world that so interested Lawrence and many other moderns. If, indeed, the old conception of ego was soon to die, if the old Victorian homocentricity was the first target of Edwardian modernism (as it seems to have been in painting and sculpture fully as much as in literature), then Hardy's allegedly old-fashioned novel is in some sense pioneering. We shall return to this issue later, but I take Husserl's method in *Ideas* to be definitive of the period between 1900 and the advent of the First World War: the modes of subjectivity, of human consciousness, are no longer viewed as "tools of distortion, of misrepresentation of an alien reality," as one contemporary philosopher puts it in attempting to characterize the Kantian position. On the contrary, the modes of consciousness properly described can become, as for Hardy, the only ancient high road to the non-human world, can, as Husserl says, "lay bare the form of the *world*," the whole world. It remained for the essentially phenomenological spirit of early modernism to dissolve the Kantian distinction between noumenal and phenomenal—to send Tess to the great monoliths of Stonehenge as a kindred spirit come home.

Two
The Return of the Native

Far more important than the much analyzed classically tragic form of *The Return of the Native* (a form which has the single conspicuous flaw that it does not work very well) is its predictable return to the great intuitions of *Far From the Madding Crowd*. Clym, even though his "newness" was apparently not prominent in Hardy's mind during the first drafts of the manuscript, has come home seeking a nature consonant with his modern deracination, abulia, and melancholy. Further, if one comes to the novel fresh from the brilliantly recast pastoralism of *Far From the Madding Crowd*, the magnificent first chapter describing the heath is more calculated than has been apparent to most readers. For one thing, it is obviously Hardy's modern pastoral.

So we must anticipate that it will be a new, modern "native" who returns to Egdon Heath and that the heath is initially described with the emotional requirements of such a modern spirit in mind. Thus Egdon seems timeless, "a face on which time makes but little impression" (to quote the title of the first chapter) and reminds one immediately of those horizon-collapsing images usually associated with Fanny Robin in the previous novel. We are told that the only way to discover this "true tale" of the heath was to see it at dusk and just before dawn, when its "somber stretch of rounds and hollows seemed to rise and meet the evening gloom in pure sympathy" (8).[1] "And so the obscurity in the air and the obscurity in the land closed together in a black fraternization towards which each advanced half-way." The distinction between sky and land is collapsed in a manner far more significant than that suggested by mere nightfall: this almost sexual union between heath and night is its "true tale," its most essential nature. And that essence is phenomenologically associated with the similar horizon-collapsing images we have already discussed.

The connection between the heath image and those surrounding Fanny's visit to Troy's barracks and her coffin's journey home introduces us to a rather seminal ontological level of Hardy's feelings about these matters. If, as I have argued in the last chapter, those images suggest a failure of relation, we had better locate the qualities that are somehow collapsed or joined in sexual union in this short chapter. Oddly enough, the answer becomes rather simple when we recognize the central paradox of these introductory pages: that although the austere heath is precisely the landscape that must appeal to a mind obsessed with "the irrepressible New," and is a landscape suggesting precisely through that untragic austerity the new sense of an indifferent cosmos replacing outworn ideals of both classical and romantic beauty, the heath is also the most permanent, inviolate, ancient, obscure, obsolete, superseded, slighted and enduring, untamable, and primitive thing under the sun. Even the remnants of an ancient highway and barrow have been "almost crystallized to natural products by long continuance" (10). Although the text suggests that the relation between "the irrepressible New" and the irrepressibly ancient is that the unaltering heath would give "ballast to the mind adrift on change, and harassed by the irrepressible New," we have come to recognize that these "collapsing" images are more threatening than that—that they disturb Hardy on a far less rational level than "ballast" would suggest.

Of course the affinity between night and the heath is not precisely the loss of all distinction that characterizes so ominously Fanny's call on Troy. Nevertheless the union of the heath with its "near relation" breeds obscurity and more obscurity. The human remains "crystallize" into something almost inseparable from the heath itself. If the heath is to provide ballast for the harassed new mentality, the more dominant image suggests that the *ur-alt* and the new are somehow lost in each other, that the key to the new is to be found in a new way of penetrating to the meaning of not just the old but of the most primitive, the unchanging beyond even the seeming permanence of landscape. Hardy carefully makes the point that Egdon is perfectly adapted for survival (in a very Darwinian way): "Those surfaces were neither so steep as to be destructible by weather, nor so flat as to be the victim of floods and deposits." The "last geological change" has only managed slight "finger-touches." Hardy has been reflecting on the geology of the heath in a very phenomenological manner, adducing the essence of its permanence as a kind of infinitely modulating quality, in contrast to the emotions of some of its inhabitants and to the great, tragic heath of Emily Brontë's Cathy and Heathcliff. It is a mistake to see the heath as some kind of topographical equivalent for the tragedy in this story. On the contrary, tragedy has an intrinsic involvement with time and timing, while the heath seems almost to have escaped time and offers an emotion for the modern sensibility that Hardy at this point can scarcely name, save that it is beyond tragedy. On the whole, then, it is curious that Hardy should have so loaded this novel with parallels to classical tragedy, when at the outset we are encouraged to pass beyond.

In sensing that the antidote to the ache of modernism lies in understanding the past in a new way, Hardy was very much aligned with the anthropology, geology, and psychology of his day, if not slightly in advance of it. Perhaps the most revolutionary discovery, made slowly during the entire nineteenth century, was that man and the earth were far, far older than anyone had imagined. If one even entertained the possibility that Darwin was right, the almost unimaginable stretch of time necessary for natural selection to produce species demanded an entirely new state of mind. The scale of things had changed. One has the feeling even while watching Milton contemplate the immensities of the creation of the universe that nonetheless his mind had not been stretched in the manner required of Hardy, Conrad, Tennyson, R. L. Stevenson, and other late Victorians. Once out of Milton's timeless heaven and potentially timeless Eden, the biblical history, however ancient, begins at once and at a rapid pace. We are not required to imagine the eons of warm seas which were man's most ancient home. It is one thing to imagine a God who always was, and quite another to imagine a man so old that as he recedes into the past he loses his identity among "lower" forms of life. It is stretching an argument only slightly to say that one of the newest things in the nineteenth century was the paleontological and geological past that had been so agonizingly uncovered.

Thus in this first chapter the primordial heath is less a possible ballast for the returning Clym's modern anguish than it is a modern and melancholy Walden, offering not transcendentalism but an acute immanentism; the meaning of the modern is found in its continuities with a past that was unimaginable before Lyell and Darwin. Clym returns, as he himself says, to rediscover what is essential in life and to strip away the very luxuries of life, thought, and feeling that Eustacia longs for with all her heart. In this surgical procedure the heath will eventually speak to him not of the difference between "the irrepressible New" and the past but of their identity. The true story of the heath is of the collapse of this particular distinction.

That Hardy is thinking in terms of the time span suggested by evolutionary processes (and by the unique quality this gives the remote past) is suggested by his description of the reddleman early in the second chapter as "of a class rapidly becoming extinct in Wessex, filling at present in the rural world the place which during the last century, the dodo occupied in the world of animals. He is a curious, interesting, and nearly perished link between the obsolete forms of life and those which generally prevail" (11). The reddleman has chosen this profession almost perversely, and perhaps with some intuitive desire to be, if only for a few years, the kind of link Hardy mentions. Diggory is archaic in his determined loyalty and willingness to play the nemesis to those who deserve it. He will step into the modern world, but reluctantly and not yet.

It is Hardy's own mention of the forms of life "which generally prevail" that stimulates thoughts of the heath as a pre-eminently well-adapted creature, largely through the slow, quiet doggedness of its existence. Insofar as Diggory is truly a creature of the heath, his mode of existence and that of the heath are similar. The heath lives with the "apparent repose of incredible slowness. A condition of healthy life so nearly resembling the torpor of death is a noticeable thing of its sort; to exhibit the inertness of the desert, and at the same time to be exercising powers akin to those of the meadow, and even of the forest, awakened in those who thought of it the attentiveness usually engendered by understatement and reserve" (15). To live at this richly subdued pace is to live forever and to live without—presumably—tragedy. Great geological cataclysms are not for Egdon. Furthermore, the rather tedious insistence (for the last page and a half of the chapter) on the organic unity of the gently rising heights, the barrow, and the single figure standing atop all, may suggest that at least some forms of human existence are consonant and even sympathetic with the heath's special mode of existence. One feels, as elsewhere when Hardy portrays these ancient barrows and rings, that the "Celts" were to his way of thinking far more closely attuned to their surroundings than subsequent cultures. In his essay on the need for preserving Stonehenge, Hardy is aware that Salisbury plain has not always looked as open as it did in his own day, yet he is struck by the fine and unnameable appropriateness of the structures to the surroundings.[2] Had Clym been able to absorb the heath's mode as the ancient Celts may have (their structures seem to "crystallize" naturally into the scene), he might not have loved Eustacia and the ache of his modernism might well have been healed by the slow, natural rhythms of a "creature" that has survived the eons. And he would not have been Clym.

Often the heath seems to suggest to Hardy the biological or botanical and geological analog of a strangely altered classical otium—beyond it, perhaps: a stoical attitude that would be as well-adapted as the heath for survival. The otium which in Gabriel Oak would be a rich content-ment, slow and natural in its unfolding, becomes in *The Return of the Native* an austere refusal of extremes, but survives as an identifiable otium nonetheless.

Eustacia is established as a genuine antithesis to the heath in all its re-lated meanings. Where it is stoic, she is tragic; where it survives, she as-pires to burn out with a great passion; where it ignores time, she likes to stare at the sand running out in her small hourglass; where its botany and geology all seem tuned to avoid great conflicts, she courts them perversely. The heath accommodates, Eustacia violates. The heath has pre-eminently adjusted to its place in nature, Eustacia refuses hers in society and delights in flaunting its conventions: on hated Sundays she does housework and hums Saturday-night ballads; "On Saturday nights she would frequently sing a psalm, and it was always on a weekday that she read the Bible, that she might be unoppressed with a sense of doing her duty" (61). She sides with the Philistines in schoolyard battles and, in a sentence that must be one of the most amusing Hardy ever wrote, "wondered if Pontius Pilate were as handsome as he was frank and fair" (60). Hardy summarizes her mind as forswearing "compromise" and adds that if we are philosophically attracted to such boldness, "it is apt to be dangerous to the commonwealth" (61). He is speaking of various sorts of commonwealth (not merely the body politic) and invites extrapolation to the Darwinian concept of adaptation. Eustacia is pre-eminently nonadaptive, and in this she is "divine" in the manner of the capricious old gods. Pagan, Corfiote, with the lip curves of old Greek statues, given to fits of melancholy and great excitement and passion, she is born to die tragically as surely as the heath will survive sto-ically. She aspires to enter the great world, but more precisely she aspires to the Dionysian fulfillment of personality.

In this fundamental opposition between Eustacia and the heath we have one of the more interesting permutations of the otium/aspiring mind di-chotomy, and the heath and Clym and Eustacia have a good deal to do with the old pastoral. Eustacia sees her drive for an all-consuming passion as a kind of "ambition" in the long tradition of the aspiring mind. She admon-ishes Wildeve (whose first name is appropriately Damon): "Damon, you have not acted well; you have sunk in my opinion. You have not valued my courtesy—the courtesy of a lady in loving you—who used to think of far more ambitious things" (71). There should be no romantic confusion about

Eustacia's motives: she is a very ambitious and aspiring woman. Clearly, having conceived this aspect of her character, Hardy had to alter Clym somewhat to make him less obviously the disillusioned philosopher returning for survival to the pastoral world and more nearly, to her eyes, the successful and fashionable, if slightly Byronic, denizen of the great world caught while slumming. It is to Hardy's credit that he could see raw ambition in so intensely romantic an aspiration without diminishing the force and tragedy of it.

There is in Eustacia a considerable inheritance from the degenerating tradition of sensibility. In the manner of Sue Bridehead, she reminds me less of Emma Bovary than of the "man of feeling" who contemplates with pleasure the fact that he is feeling, and with more intensity and finesse than the ordinary folk around him. When Wildeve assures Eustacia that he will never "wish" to desert her, she replies:

> "I do not thank you for that. I should hate it to be all smooth. Indeed, I think I like you to desert me a little once now and then. Love is the dismallest thing where the lover is quite honest. O, it is a shame to say so; but it is true!" She indulged in a little laugh. "My low spirits begin at the very idea. Don't you offer me tame love, or away you go!" (71)

Even in her most distraught moments, there seems always to be an aesthetic distance between Eustacia's feelings and her consciousness of them. Like most suicides (or so psychologists tell us) she may want to see herself as a suicide almost as much as she wants to contemplate herself loving greatly. We must remember that throughout this interview with Wildeve, the reddleman is listening, unobserved because he has almost completely covered himself with heath turves. He has literally become part of the heath, while they affirm their "hate" for it and Eustacia argues that it is her "cross, my shame, and will be my death!" Its very mode of existence is antipathetic to hers: as the reddleman lifts the turves and watches the black figures of Eustacia and Wildeve against the sky, they appear "as two horns which the sluggish heath had put forth from its crown, like a mollusk, and had now again drawn in" (74).

How entirely misleading to see Egdon heath as an echo of Emily Brontë's tortured and romantic landscape, as do many of us who remember it at a distance of ten or twenty years. The heath does not echo or underwrite the tragic aspirations of Eustacia but seems instead to negate them. It is "sluggish"—quite the slowly surviving nemesis, somewhat in the way that the reddleman is to the story, and much as his trade is, to use the anthropological term, a "survival." The mollusk image suggests that even these two, at least one of whom is a passionately aspiring "feeler," are ontologically subsumed by another order of existence. The heath endures at least partly because it is so archaically fundamental—beyond and beneath even the most intense human feelings and certainly beyond Eustacia's fine scrutiny of her feelings. It is as though Hardy is intimating that evolution has finally produced a creature who is too determinedly self-reflective and (in feelings riddled with self-consciousness) too artificial to survive. The mollusks survive, the heath survives, Diggory survives. All this artificiality in Eustacia, of course, calls into question the possibility of real tragedy for her. The old Greek tragic heroes did not avidly pursue their self-images as tragic heroes. They felt their tragedy immediately and without the intervention of an almost literary self-image: "In emotion she was all the while an epicure" (8).

That Eustacia should use the ancient Rainbarrow and ceremonial fires as the trappings of her on-and-off romantic enthusiasm for Wildeve somehow fits her appropriation of the mummer's role as a means of catching a glimpse of Clym. In describing the mummers as a "survival" (102), Hardy is using a word crucial to understanding his attitude toward the past. It is not irrelevant, then, that Eustacia is rather strangely described as having "the greatest contempt" for "mummers and mumming" (102). Why "the greatest contempt"? No really adequate explanation is ever given, except that the mummers are part of the rustic isolation she feels on the heath, so that mumming and the heath are joined in her mind. More important, though Hardy never discusses the issue directly, is the obvious linking of the ancient mumming with the even more ancient survival qualities of the heath, the barrows, the ceremonial fires. Eustacia intuitively hates the mumming because it is involved with the mode of existence that apparently undercuts her own. And this is not alone to say that the stoic, accommodating toughness of the heath is opposed to her propensity for short-lived destructive tragedy: the heath and all other "survivals" in this novel contradict precisely the emotional epicureanism and artificiality of Eustacia. Though hard to recognize, she is a further refinement of the almost surreal artificiality that Clym has fled in Paris and the diamond business. She seeks

out Clym not as a unique individual whom she will love because of what
he is, but as a likely candidate for the role her imagination has created
despite what he is, namely a man in love with the heath and the survivals
and all they mean.

Hardy knows better than most how perfunctory many of these survivals are.

> A traditional pastime is to be distinguished from a mere revival in
> no more striking feature than this, that while in the revival all is
> excitement and fervour, the survival is carried on with a stolidity
> and absence of stir which sets one wondering why a thing that is
> done so perfunctorily should be kept up at all. Like Balaam and
> other unwilling prophets, the agents seem moved by an inner com-
> pulsion to say and do their allotted parts whether they will or no.
> This unweeting manner of performance is the true ring by which,
> in this refurbishing age, a fossilized survival may be known from a
> spurious reproduction. (102–3)

I quote this passage at length because it is one of the most likely to be
misread in the entire novel. Hardy is not gently satirizing those who
numbly continue those traditions and suggesting that such things may as
well be dropped. The word "fossilized" is invariably misleading to a reader
who has not begun to recapture the excitement that fossils created in the
nineteenth century. Of course the whole passage is laced together with
irony, but the "stolidity" with which the "survival" is presented is sterility
only to the unsympathetic viewer. In fact Hardy's irony throughout is designed to capture the urbane scepticism of one of the creatures of the "re-
furbishing age."

But this "stolidity and absence of stir" with which the mummers perform suggests something of the survival quality of the heath, the barrows,
the fires, and the mumming itself. Like the May "walking" which opens
Tess of the d'Urbervilles, these ceremonies contain a power that survives
the perfunctoriness that modern man often unconsciously uses to disguise
their frightening significance. If competition in decorating the costumes
leaves Saint George looking pretty much like the "deadly enemy," the
Saracen, it is Hardy who reminds us of the archaic meaning by having
the "pagan" Eustacia play the Turkish Knight. Eustacia is antithetical to all

the potentially deep continuity represented by these survivals, however disguised and distorted they may have become. Hardy had for them a tremendous respect that far transcends any notion of mere nostalgia and probably went far deeper into his major aesthetic concerns than even he could articulate. If the great signal fires of the autumnal equinox, with, as Hardy says, all their Promethean meaning and their role in the profound cycles of birth and death and rebirth, are today disguised by some ersatz association with the Powder Plot, the feelings and actions which these fires precipitate have no difficulty blending harmoniously with the lives of those who built the great barrow and the bonfires of the past.

When Eustacia, however, plays the Turkish Knight, she rants the words with only a superficial resemblance to the way the role is usually played. "Like in form, it had the added softness and finish of a Raffaelle after Perugino, which, while faithfully reproducing the original subject, entirely distances the original art" (105). Eustacia stands against the meaning of the heath and of the "survivals" largely because she characteristically has this refining, epicurean, overcivilizing if antisocial quality to her every thought and action. Of course Raphael studied and imitated Perugino (one recalls Berenson's comment, "At whose feet did he not sit?"). But Raphael almost immediately refines away the utterly pristine, pastoral elegance of a Perugino.

The "ranting" of the mummers is a truly primitive, compulsive prophecy, coming in all its rote and outward stolidity from the most fundamental wellsprings of European experience: the Western tradition challenged by an alien culture, light by darkness. The mummers do not understand this, they transmit it. Eustacia's intuitive refining and softening of the whole performance is precisely the only thing in the performance with the unmistakable hint of denial in it. The mummery has survived in a manner reminiscent of the heath's: it has been able to accommodate all the fancy costumes and blurring of characters without losing its basic identity. Can there be any doubt, however, that the coming of people such as Eustacia is the beginning of the end? Her refining "entirely distances the original art," as a Raphael does the pristine Perugino. It is the same aesthetic distance that we find lying ominously between her feelings and her consciousness of them. The decadence is truly that seen so exaggeratedly in the "man of feeling" and in the decline of the tradition of sensibility. The supreme irony is that the only man who can see the importance of these survivals (as he does of the heath-life) and possibly interpret them as some kind of priest-philosopher, is precisely the man she now hunts for the lead role in her romantic passion.

I do not mean to cast Eustacia as some ultimate in decadent sophistication. Quite the contrary, she is in many ways entirely naive, and Clym is supposed to be the world-weary sophisticate. Her role in quickly seeing to it that Wildeve marries Thomasin is, however, anything but ingenuous and must rank with other high points of cynical opportunism in the English novel. The reddleman is the only innocent person in the entire affair, coldly used by all concerned, even Thomasin herself. Eustacia's naiveté is an elusive quality hard to attribute to any one of her characteristics and yet most intimately associated with her pervasive faith in the satisfaction to be had through great passion. She is innocent of the knowledge that causes definitively modern melancholy in Clym, that makes his worn face the new standard of beauty, "the typical countenance of the future" (139). She at least has an innocent faith in the efficacy of *some* kind of human emotion.

It is not in Eustacia's dread of the heath that this novel gives us great symbolic difficulty but in Clym's love for it. The paradox is simply this: he is the true child of the heath ("permeated with its scene, with its substance, and with its odors. He might be said to be its product" [144]); yet he is also Hardy's embodiment, in this novel, of all that is modern. Even his childhood toys had been "the flint knives and arrowheads which he found there, wondering why stones should 'grow' to such odd shapes" (144). To many, Hardy says, "this Egdon was a place which had slipped out of its century generations ago, to intrude as an uncouth object into this. It was an obsolete thing, and few cared to study it" (144). It is, in short, another of the "survivals" that so interest Hardy. Our paradox, more precisely, is that anyone so entirely modern as Clym should also be the very child of this ancient thing and react with "barbarous satisfaction" at seeing some of the attempts to farm the heath fail. If Clym, sickened and disillusioned at the modern life he has seen, were returning to the heath for all its ancient survival values, we should understand at once. But, strangely enough, Clym's modernity and his identity as a true child of the ancient heath seem to be very similar in Hardy's mind. Clym may return to the essentials of rustic life and heath-existence in flight from the "idlest, vainest, most effeminate business that ever a man could be put to" (142), but there is nothing in the heath that can cure the anguish of his modernity. In a very surprising sense, Clym's intimate knowledge of the heath and its meaning serves to *confirm* the assorted knowledge that constitutes his modernity. Ancient and modern are conflated, *if* we appreciate that in the heath the idea of the past has been given a new dimension by Hardy.

As the sensate being that Hardy's imagery continually makes it, the heath "knows" the "defects of natural laws" (139), that brilliantly succinct phrase that sums up so much of the late-Victorian predicament; and the heath survives by its own "wild and ascetic" ways (140), the key to the whole pattern of survival being ascetic and yet strategic endurance. Both the heath and Clym are definitively ascetic and understated. As he tells his mother when she asks him why he cannot accept a life of self-indulgence as well as others can:

> "I don't know, except that there are many things other people care for which I don't; and that's partly why I think I ought to do this. For one thing, my body does not require much of me. Well, I ought to turn that defect to advantage, and being able to do without what other people require I can spend what such things cost upon anybody else." (146)

This is an ascetic faith that, except for its spirit of sacrifice, might almost be the motto of the heath as a geological and biological entity. After all, the phrase "wild and ascetic" that I used above was evoked by Hardy to describe the young Clym, but in a context that makes it clear his peculiar kind of wildness and asceticism are heath-born. To complete another of the contrasts that lie at the core of this tragedy, we need only remember that Eustacia is a peculiarly self-indulgent woman in the manner of decadent sensibility that I have outlined. The apparent austerity of the heath, as much as its loneliness and wildness, is what alienates her.

Yet the slow, even sluggish asceticism of the heath and Clym is possibly the way to cope with the knowledge they both seem to have of existence. As a survival, the heath reveals the means of its survival, and two of its ancient artifacts are made to bear the modern flower, the emblem itself of the ability to survive toughly on almost nothing: "The only visible articles in the room [Eustacia's] were those on the window-sill, which showed their shapes against the low sky: the middle article being the old hour-glass, and the other two a pair of ancient British urns which had been dug from a barrow near, and were used as flower-pots for two razor-leaved cactuses" (102). This is one of the most powerful images in the entire novel, the hourglass having been used earlier to signal Eustacia's impatience with time in contrast to the slow, almost timeless quality that Hardy invariably associates with the sheer stamina of survivals.

That these "razor-leaved cactuses" should grow in the urns, the ancient British urns, suggests a distinction in Hardy's mind between the usefulness for the modern British sensibility of the Hellenic past and the native, British past. The Hellenic is dead:

> The truth seems to be that a long line of disillusive centuries has permanently displaced the Hellenic idea of life, or whatever it may be called. What the Greeks only suspected we know well; what their Aeschylus imagined our nursery children feel. The old-fashioned reveling in the general situation grows less and less possible as we uncover the defects of natural laws, and see the quandary that man is in by their operation. (138)

Even the Hellenic ideal of beauty has lost relevance. Hardy contends that "the view of life as a thing to be put up with" has replaced "that zest for existence which was so intense in early civilizations" (139), all of which may suggest an irony in these cactuses growing from the urns (albeit that they are probably funerary) of a presumably zestful earlier civilization. The persistent reference to the consonance of the early British barrows and remains with the heath itself, however, would suggest that while the Roman legions hurried to be clear of Egdon by November, fearing its dismal ambience, there were natives who understood and built their barrows in such a way that they seemed the natural culmination of the scene. Clym is the direct heir of these earlier natives.

If one is uncomfortable in pursuing the close resemblance of Clym and the heath it is probably because some critics have made much of the fact that while the heath presents a face unaffected by time, Clym's face is "modern" precisely because it is so thoroughly and symbolically the record of his disillusionment. Such observations ignore, however, the early reference to "haggard Egdon" (8) and Hardy's claim that "like man" the heath is "slighted and enduring." The heath is "obscure, obsolete" and "superseded" (9). Clearly Hardy meant to imply that Clym's modern knowledge consists primarily in realizing not only that neither the universe nor its laws were made for man but that man feels slighted by whatever universal plan may emerge from the discoveries of modern science. Man is a "survival," as the heath, mummery, and November Fifth bonfires are.

And like the mummery, for example, he possesses a potential power that far transcends the apparent rote of his existence. Just as the power of the May walking in *Tess of the d'Urbervilles* or the fires or mummery in *The Return of the Native* can be released by probing their incredible antiquity, so man by beginning to discover his antiquity may release an unheard-of potential within himself. But of course the antiquity that must be approached is unlike anything that any century before the nineteenth knew about. Now we are in a position to understand why Hardy should have reported that his blood ran cold when the Maumbury Ring was discovered to have paleolithic origins. If in probing the most remote origins of "St. George and the Dragon" the anthropologically minded can discover primitive rituals concerning the birth, death, and rebirth of the seasons, so man in his capacity as a survival (slighted, enduring, obscure, and obsolete) can probe within himself for an analogous meaning.

This quality of being slighted and regarded as obsolete is at the roots of Hardy's respect and sympathy for the literally hundreds of survivals he records so lovingly in his novels and poems. Like them, man exists a seeming stranger in the new universe that Victorian science had made—somewhat old-fashioned, enigmatic, but above all carrying a runic message to be read only by those who sense its far from superseded power. It is no exaggeration to say that all Hardy's art comes around eventually to the problem of understanding man against the background of an antiquity that had earlier in the century made biblical accounts of creation and genealogy seem like yesterday, and that always for Hardy made Roman England seem the very top of that blood-chilling excavation to man's origins. When Clym tells Eustacia that there is "a very curious Druidical stone" on the heath and assumes she must often go to see it, she replies that she knows of no such stone: "I am aware that there are Boulevards in Paris" (155). They separate a moment later, and Hardy says that under the prospect of their coming great passion, "her past was a blank, her life had begun" (155). Her "blank" past, in contrast with Clym's desire to read the runic meaning of man's survival, to possess a past so vast and symbolic that we are still struggling with its emotional impact one hundred years later, provides the true conflict and tragedy of this novel. Eustacia is not only a lover but his nemesis on this most important issue of his life.

Hardy's intuitive identification of man himself as a survival, in the most far-reaching late-nineteenth-century sense of that word, is a metaphor of incalculable importance. It destroys at once any notion that Hardy's taste for these rustic ceremonies, words, and customs was merely nostalgia or an attempt to live a moment longer in a pastoral world far from perfect but infinitely preferable to the one aborning. It explodes any notion of the heath as Sartrean "in-itself" and Clym and Eustacia as somehow tragically fated "for-itself" consciousness, finally confronted with the ultimate nemesis of indifferent matter. If both the heath and man are survivals, the description of them as Ishmaelitish grows in importance.

It is the fate of Ishmael (though only the son of Abraham and a slave) to be disinherited by Sarah for the benefit of her own son Isaac. The distance from Melville's "Call me Ishmael" to the Ishmaelitish heath and heath "native" is not so great as the gap of twenty-seven years and a world of American experience might suggest. The anthropological survival is by definition disinherited and cast into the wilderness of a foreign time, where it will not be understood and its runic message may become merely picturesque. If man in Hardy's eyes is also a survival, it is because he finds himself outliving the divinely ordered universe in which his place was primary. In the new universe, his longing for an ethical purpose to creation and for a meaningful role within it is outdated, obsolete, even quaint from some positivist perspectives. And like Ishmael, the new man finds himself in a wilderness specifically in having lost whatever favor or inheritance he might have had. The nineteenth-century Ishmael, be he Melville's or Hardy's, lies under the curse of being a wild man (as does the biblical figure) in the sense of needing to become a kind of philosophic hero who, cast out of one orderly world, must ask the most disruptive questions in order to make a new one.

In losing the inheritance and favor of an earlier world view (involving, no doubt, some Emersonian correspondence of appearance and reality), Melville's Ishmael must virtually go back to epistemological origins. There are no longer any guidelines for moving from the phenomenal to the noumenal world, nor any guarantee in the world of appearance that a noumenal world lies behind it at all. Even the idea that the world of the senses was somehow a product of the Fall (and thus that the senses were deceptive, misleading, and even the instruments of the devil) was a guarantee of noumenal reality to a good many Puritan sensibilities, who proceeded at their crudest to reverse the sense data in order to arrive at the real. I think it is possible to see that Hardy makes Clym a kind of would-be wild man not only in his taste for the most rudimentary heath-life but in his somewhat optimistic desire to reexamine the meanings of life in the most fundamental way.

It appears, however, that Hardy has once more given us some of the old pastoral spirit for grasping Clym's attempt to live in the wilderness of the new scepticism. After all, the implication of a survival is that it conceals an important meaning which can be evoked if we understand its original context. Thus, when Hardy remarks that the mumming of St. George ends with nobody commenting any more than they "would have commented on the fact of mushrooms coming in autumn or snowdrops in spring" (116), he may be intimating that the survival just performed had almost the same level of significance as vegetative rebirth and cycle. Does it follow that man may be the only survival who bears no such important meaning, in the sense that the old context in which he had meaning is *absolutely* discredited (i.e., that an ethically and divinely ordered universe is simply a lie)?

The term "survival" was first used by E. B. Tylor in his 1871 *Primitive Culture* (London: J. Murray),[3] a title which turns up in Hardy's *Literary Notes* while he summarizes a passage from Herbert Spencer. There is no hint that Hardy had read Tylor's earlier *Anahuas or Mexico and the Mexicans, Ancient and Modern* of 1861 or the more important *Researches into the Early History of Mankind and the Development of Civilization* of 1865, but the evidence of *The Return of the Native* suggests that he had almost certainly become familiar by the early 1870s with the importance of the concept of survivals to evolutionist method. As Tylor said in 1871,

> These are processes, customs, opinions and so forth which have been carried on by force of habit into a new state of society different from that in which they had their original home, and they thus remain as proofs and examples of an older condition of culture out of which a newer has been evolved.[4]

Hardy may even have read or heard of John Lubbock's *The Origin of Civilization* (London: Longman Green, 1870) or his earlier *Pre-Historic*

Times, as Illustrated by Ancient Remains and the Manners and Customs of Modern Savages (London: Williams and Norgate, 1865), since Lubbock was to my knowledge the only early evolutionary anthropologist who both pioneered the study of survivals and at great length claimed that Fetishism was the earliest stage of the evolution of religion, which then grew through Nature Worship, Shamanism, and Idolatry on to a modern conception of God as "the author, not merely a part, of nature."[5] In trying to describe the complex November sound of the heath as the "united product of infinitesimal vegetable causes," of the wind entering the "mummied" heath bells, Hardy concludes:

> The spirit moved them. A meaning of the phrase forced itself upon the attention; and an emotional listener's fetichistic mood might have ended in one of more advanced quality. It was not, after all, that the left-hand expanse of old brooms spoke, or the right-hand, or those of the slope in front; but it was the single person of something else speaking through each at once. (47)

This "evolution" is really an unmistakable period piece which could have been influenced by Tylor's description of the evolution of religion in *Primitive Culture* (1871) but, with its emphasis on fetishism as a distinct stage which we "advance" beyond, is more characteristic of Lubbock and would not again be entirely characteristic of another such theory until Frazer and *The Golden Bough* (1890) or *Totemism* (1887). Suffice it to say that Tylor's evolution of religious feeling is a far subtler theory that does not offer fetishism as a distinct stage at all. In fact, Hardy's passage seems to note rather precisely (and somewhat ironically) that moment when the mind seems to "progress" from seeing spirit *in* nature to feeling that some noumenal presence beyond nature is simply speaking through the various natural details of the heath. For Lubbock this was the most important moment in the evolution of religion, though he would have suggested three or four more stages between fetishism and any such realization.

Comte and Herbert Spencer, though not exactly evolutionary anthropologists, were very much interested in fetishism as a stage in the development, the evolution, of their religion of mankind. Hardy's *Literary Notes* contains annotated passages from Comte and Spencer in which fetishism and the evolution of religious feeling are precisely the issue, although Spencer as we might expect is using his view of fetishism to attack the positivist position. There are uses of the term and the idea of fetishism often enough in *Tess of the d'Urbervilles* to suggest that if Hardy had discovered the word in translations of Comte, he thought of it in connection with that not unrelated evolutionary spirit infusing both things and people in that novel. When Hardy's friend Frederic Harrison awkwardly suggested to Hardy that *Tess* "reads like a Positivist allegory or sermon," he had at least applied a popular term to Hardy's very personal tendency in the novel toward a form of synthesizing consciousness that will be the subject of another chapter. Although the "progress" and positivist method implicit in all Comte's writing was uncongenial to Hardy, the idea of a talismanic power inhering in things seemed to fascinate Hardy as some kind of access to man's deepest archaism. Elsewhere in the *Literary Notes* Hardy summarizes a passage from Herbert Spencer's *Principles of Biology* (London, 1864), in which Spencer argues that "it cannot be said that inanimate things present no parallels to animate ones."[6]

Whether it may be Lubbock or Comte or Spencer in the background here is relatively unimportant. Hardy is in any event demonstrating that he comes to *The Return of the Native* full of recent anthropological orientations and queries and that foremost in his mind is the issue of survivals so important to Tylor's *Primitive Culture*. We have at last, I think, an explanation for the crescendo of interest in survivals (including his use of the term itself) in this novel. Hardy had of course always been interested in old folkways, but in *The Return of the Native* he suddenly has a conceptual frame that both contributes to and extensively modifies the old pastoral ensemble of language and attitudes so important to *Far From the Madding Crowd*.

All through the 1860s and at least since Lewis Henry Morgan's *League of the Ho-de-no-sau-nee, or Iroquois* (Rochester: Sage and Bros., 1851), the idea of survivals had been part of the intellectual climate. H. S. Maine and J. F. McLennan had discussed the problem with regard to marriage (*Primitive Marriage*, Edinburgh: Adam and Charles Black, 1865) and law (*Ancient Law*, London: J. Murray, 1861), and of course Darwin himself had provided biological models for the anthropological ploy in 1859. One is not to assume, however, that the biological model was fundamental in the discovery and use of survivals as an important part of the comparative method. Their prominence during this crucial period of 1851 through 1878 (to use the date of *The Return of the Native*) was undoubtedly due to changes in mental habits even more fundamental than those occasioned by Darwin—changes having to do with a dawning realization of the way the past could lie *in* the present and of the ultrabiblical antiquity of the past. No doubt the spirit of Lyell was equally moving to Hardy, for the man is epitomized by a single unidentified quotation in the *Literary Notes*: "*The enthusiasm* of Sir Charles Lyell, who when travelling along a cutting gazed out of the railway carriage as if the sides were hung with beautiful pictures" (1078).

Incredibly, then, not only the bonfires, the mumming, and so on, are survivals, but the heath and man himself are conceived of in this great anthropological vein. Survivals were used by these evolutionary anthropologists to reconstruct the antecedent stages of cultural evolution, and when such method came under attack by modern relativist anthropologists, it was by means of challenging the uselessness that men such as Tylor were alleged to have seen in survivals. A modern "functionalist" anthropologist would claim that in calling a particular activity a survival (and therefore functionless in its present context), Tylor and his followers had paid insufficient attention to the ways such apparently atrophied practices have assumed new and often subtle functions in the new culture. As Marvin Harris points out in his discussion of the problem,[7] such attacks completely misrepresent the customary use of survivals by evolutionary anthropologists, who did not regard "uselessness" in the survivals' present context as an essential part of the definition.

Hardy, as he often does, anticipates this most subtle crux of modern anthropological method by intimating at considerable length that the ceremony of the fires, though its ancient religious or ritual context no longer holds, continues as the answer to some basic, human, Promethean need to defy the coming of winter's darkness as well as of some kind of psychic darkness. Indeed, Hardy characteristically refuses to see any of the hundreds of survivals that fill his novels (especially from *The Return of the Native* on) as defined by their being useless or purposeless in the present context. It is easy enough to see that they emerge from a time when their details would have had a ready explanation; but on the whole Hardy's point is that they survive, often if not invariably, because they reach a human need that transcends changes in culture, or at least all but the most seminal changes in culture. Hardy had apparently no great faith that some uniform evolutionary pattern would be discovered for culture, as it either had been or would be for biological man. Thus he is deliberately a bit facile when he mentions the "advance" from the fetishistic stage or when he uses some variation of Morgan's stages of savagery, barbarism, and civilization. But he is nonetheless willing, as few of his contemporary novelists were, to proceed from the evidence of survivals of all kinds to a diachronic sense of man's identity that far surpassed the most elaborate synchronic definitions of his day. Hardy was better than most at placing his characters in a rich, synchronic social context, even to the extent of relating neighborhoods to counties, districts, and regions; families to crossroads, towns, and cities; and so and on in the manner demonstrated so brilliantly in Tess's endless walks and in his discussions of Casterbridge in *The Mayor of Casterbridge*. But it was to the past, largely through the whole concept of a survival, that Hardy turned, expecting to discover not the laws of culture's evolution but the qualities in man that survive the alteration of culture.

Clym and Hardy, however, part company on just this issue of what it is of inestimable value that the survivals may reveal. Fascinated as he is by the old folkways, when Eustacia is jabbed with a hat pin in church, Clym declares that he has "come to clear away those cobwebs" (154), to educate the heath people away from their irrational superstitions. He would, on the whole, try to give them a rational view of their place in creation that would stoically equip them to bear the vale of tears. He says to Eustacia, "There is no use in hating people—if you hate anything you should hate what produced them" (154). No doubt Clym means ignorance, superstition, and a generally irrational approach to life. Yet Eustacia answers him immediately with a comment that must represent the measure of Hardy's ironic distance from Clym: "Do you mean Nature? I hate her already." It has not occurred to Clym that Nature is in some sense the source of both the best qualities in the survivals *and* Susan Nunsuch's belief in witches.

If we follow the analysis of survivals back toward some primitive essence of man, rationality is not what we discover. Clym's "high thinking" seems to ignore the quality of his own intimate relationship with the heath. Though apparently Clym believes a kind of rational stoicism will prove the best survival quality he can offer the heath people, these "clowns" (143) already survive pretty well with an irrationality which, if it produces superstition and Susan Nunsuch with her needle, has also produced in its symbiotic, even mythic and ritualistic capacity the continuity of the survivals themselves.

The great fires which begin the novel are the perfect example. They are important both to Hardy and the rustics who year after year create them for more than a moderately pleasant social event. They are as much "prophetic" and capable of affecting Hardy on an inarticulate, almost impersonal level as some of the survivals that were to fascinate Morgan, Tylor, Frazer, and finally a whole panoply of modern artists (and of these last, even some great ones could never entirely believe that Madam Sosostris's pack of cards was a dead and debased mystery to the modern world, or that those dried currants would never more speak of Dionysus and the fertility cults). The continuity with the past that would have been so sustaining to T. S. Eliot was not a rational matter so much as it was chthonic and spiritual. Eliot was able to involve Christianity in these other, more ancient ritual survivals; Hardy does not and did not even try. To the heath people, as to the rustics of *Far From the Madding Crowd*, Christianity is largely a social issue or the basis for rather comic discussions about high church and low church. Almost nobody manages to get to church in *The Return of the Native*, and when Eustacia finally does arrive she is immediately the victim of pagan superstition.

Hardy was never certain whether the lives of these heath people were really sustained to any degree by their involvement in the hundreds of pagan survivals that weave in and out of their existence. Surely they are more involved in the old pagan ways than in the Christian, but Hardy is never certain that he can attribute to the natives even an intuitive participation in the meaning of these survivals. *Meaning*, however, is a quasi-rational term that we need not impose on the obvious *involvement* of these people in the great symbolic cycles and rhythms of existence that make Clym's high thinking seem the most arrogant presumption.

In short, if we follow these survivals back to the earlier world view and "stage" of human culture that they imply, we recover not a *discredited* and now useless view of a noumenously significant Nature, but an original state of mind which, Hardy would like to say, has a truth of its own. The question is, can he bring himself to claim such a usefulness? He is trapped in a dilemma in which the "truth" of modern science seems to demand that, on one hand, we discredit the various ritualistic and mythic ways in which the natural world seems pregnant with human relevance, though, on the other, these great mythic meanings call to us as they called to T. S. Eliot and D. H. Lawrence and Yeats and Joyce. This ambivalence is rather nicely embodied in Hardy's attitude toward Clym's missionary zeal. He is both the child of the heath and the stepson of modern skepticism; sustained by his Antaeus-like dependence on the heath, he would yet bring to its inhabitants the gifts of his rationalism, a rationalism whose consequences have driven him back to the heath in the first place.

The stance Hardy is slowly working toward seems to involve the loss of a pride that demands of Nature more than man's equal participation in these great rhythms and sympathies. If rationalism and the heightened self-consciousness it encourages demand a natural world with a human ethical rationale, we shall be eternally and definitively frustrated—tragic or pathetic creatures depending on our degree of ego and presumption. If, on the contrary, we allow the survivals to help take us back to a time and state of mind where one does not feel the necessity of imposing human ethics on natural order, a certain kind of peace may be possible: and this peace may be the ultimate otium, the new otium consonant with the demands of the new pastoral. But Hardy's question is always whether such loss of pride, such peace, is really compatible with consciousness itself—whether it is not in the essence of consciousness, especially self-consciousness, to be always outside these rhythms and thus instinctively critical of them. A similar problem lies at the very core of D. H. Lawrence's best work.

It is, after all, one thing to be at peace—and nearly absorbed—by the Nature of the old pastoral and quite another to yield to a truly diachronic nature extending back and beyond the "carboniferous" age, where no birds sing and the soft ferns seem "machine-made foliage, a world of green triangles with saw-edges, and not a single flower" (169). This famous passage is simply another one of those moments when the entire idea of the natural world is suddenly brutalized as much by a knowledge of the mechanics of evolution as by the sheer meaning of an incredibly extended antiquity. If we are to yield to the much earlier state of mind discussed above, will we not discover that this natural world is itself a kind of hidden mechanism that in its early, most revealing periods produced its true image in "machine-made foliage" with its ominous "saw-edges" and "monotonous extent of leafage" (169)? Hardy is infinitely attracted to this new otium yet deeply fearful that the natural world is not worthy of the sacrifice involved. Is the later Clym, nearly blind and so much a part of the heath that he is at times indistinguishable from it, a better man than the clear-sighted missionary of the novel's opening? Is it a question of man coming home (possibly through some of the survivals that had allowed the evolutionary anthropologists a conceptual point of entry they had previously lacked)? Or is it more nearly true to say that the fundamental myth is not the possibility of the return of the native but whatever myth would make man not a survival but a mutation, an Ishmaelitish creature whose essence is never to have been "native" anywhere at any time? *The Return of the Native* questions the viability not so much of the word *return* as of the word *native*.

That Hardy still views this larger dilemma in the context of otium and the aspiring mind is sufficiently emphasized by his continual reference to the ambition of Eustacia. Flinging himself upon the heath (actually the Rainbarrow itself), Clym watches the eclipse of the moon and waits for this prearranged signal to bring Eustacia (161). He longs to escape the aspirations of Eustacia and his mother in favor of a "world where personal ambition was not the only recognized form of progress—such, perhaps, as might have been the case at some time or other in the silvery globe then shining upon him" (161).

As Clym goes on to contemplate the topography of the moon we realize that this is an important moment in the history of the pastoral: to escape the aspiring mind (Clym's missionary goals are rather selfless) apparently necessitates an imaginative flight to the moon. From one's own vineyard to Arcady to the moon, in slightly less than two thousand years! We must travel farther and farther to flee that ancient aspiring mind. He passionately views it for a few moments as a symbol of his much-sought peace and otium, and, of course, it is the eclipse of that moon which is the signal for Eustacia's arrival. Eustacia's aspirations extend even to the eclipse of that most remote fantasy of Clym's peace. The symbolism is a bit heavy, but unmistakable. The shadow "widens" until Eustacia (whose grandfather was characteristically epic, "a sort of Greek Ulysses" [176]), falls into his arms. Her love will be the death of his dream of otium, or the total eclipse of it. We really do not know which is the more intense of Eustacia's aspirations, her taste for the great world of luxury ("luxurious" is Clym's description [165]) or for the all-consuming passion of a great love in which marriage is the ultimate boredom. Most basically understood, she aspires to seeing herself in a great love from the luxurious aesthetic distance we discussed earlier.

As Eustacia seduces him from his asceticism and dream of pastoral peace, the eclipse progresses until she says: "Clym, the eclipsed moonlight shines upon your face with a strange foreign color, and shows its shape as if it were cut out in gold. That means that you should be doing better things than this" (165). The "gold" is symbolically consonant with the meaning the scene has established for the eclipsed moon, the eclipse by her ambition of his pastoral dream ("I could live and die in a hermitage here, with proper work to do").

After the conversation in which Eustacia agrees to marry him, Clym watches her depart into a magnificent early summer landscape. He is, however, oppressed by its "horizontality which too much reminded him of the arena of life; it gave him a sense of bare equality with, and no superiority to, a single living thing under the sun" (172). But of course the survivals may lead one to just this sense of equality, and not superiority, to all life. Obviously Clym still has all the pride of intellect that may prevent him from any intuitive grasp of the archaic mind and its equal participation in the natural world. Yet his failing eyesight soon brings this "unambitious" (207) man so close, microscopically close to the intimate small life of the heath that "huge flies, ignorant of larders and wire-netting, and quite in a savage state, buzzed about him without knowing that he was a man" (207). He is happy, calm, and he sings, much to the dismay of Eustacia, who feels that a real man would rebel at this reduction in social circumstances. Presumably Clym too is experiencing at least some small touch of the "savage state," and in this frame of mind he is a long way from a Jobian outrage that the universe has not been arranged according to man's ethical standards.

The long paragraph describing the life of the butterflies, grasshoppers, flies, snakes, and rabbits that constitute Clym's field of vision is one of the most contented passages Hardy ever wrote, containing none of the outrage he ordinarily felt at man's dubious nativity. But it has taken a dire injury to get Clym to this point, and the plot-ridden section of the novel is just beginning. In it, Clym is so exhausted by tragedy and reduced by sheer chance and happenstance that it is almost as though Hardy were defending himself against a clear confrontation with the issues that crystallize immediately before all this pseudo-Greek claptrap begins.

Neither Clym nor Eustacia make very good tragic figures: Clym partly because so much of his energy is spent brooding over the death of a mother whose true nature is barely glimpsed in the falling out with her son over Eustacia. More important, however, is the reader's feeling that any tragedy appropriate to Clym must have a great deal to do with this approach to that strange, archaic otium that has been evolving throughout both *Far From the Madding Crowd* and *The Return of the Native.* In a very striking sense, Clym's alleged tragedy is nearly irrelevant to the true focus of the first two-thirds of the novel. Given the fundamental opposition of Clym and Eustacia, it might have been interesting to write a tragedy that would have told us more about the essential ontologies holding them apart. Instead the tragedy merely reiterates their incompatibility and leaves us with a "tragic" heroine whose main disappointment is that the only passionate opportunity on the horizon is breaking her marriage vows for a man, Wildeve, who "is not great enough" and "does not suffice for my desire!": "If he had been a Saul or a Bonaparte—ah! But to break my marriage vow for him—it is too poor a luxury!" (288). There must be a difference between petulance, however impassioned, and tragic grief.

The potential tragedy of *The Return of the Native* lies in the native's not being able to return, if we understand *native* and *return* in the broadly evolutionary context I have established. Hardy will not explore the question of whether Clym, thoroughly disillusioned by the aspiring world and the new science, can return to a nature newly pregnant with a hitherto inconceivable antiquity and, abandoning the ego that makes him impose human ethics on nature, reach some consonance that is not dehumanizing. We are simply told by Hardy that following his assorted tragedies, Clym on the contrary will not "construct a hypothesis that shall . . . degrade a First Cause" and like most men will not "conceive a dominant power of lower moral quality than their own" (308). He is no Job (who must be one of the "sternest of men" [308]) but comes remarkably close to being a meliorist. The great irony is that although in these days he feels closest to the ancient Celtic inhabitants of the heath and "could almost live among them, look in their faces, and see them standing beside the barrows" (309), it is Thomasin and not he who can respond to the Maypole that spring, and to its "symbolic customs" and "Teutonic rites." Hardy lovingly describes its phallic adornment with flowers and reminds us that "Thomasin noticed all these, and was delighted that the May-revel was to be so near" (313). Clym, though he later preaches from the Rainbarrow and no doubt still feels himself close to its ancient builders, has in some way slipped out of the archaic channels he had begun to enter.

Hardy takes care to indicate two entirely different kinds of involvement with the heath in these last pages. On one hand Hardy cannot think of Eustacia's intensifying antipathy to the heath without allowing his own grotesque imagination to run to extremes: "Skirting the pool she followed the path towards Rainbarrow, occasionally stumbling over twisted furze-roots, tufts of rushes, or oozing lumps of fleshy fungi, which at this season lay scattered about the heath like the rotten liver and lungs of some colossal animal. . . . She sighed bitterly and ceased to stand erect, gradually crouching down under the umbrella as if she were drawn into the barrow by a hand from beneath" (287). These bizarre animations of the heath and barrow are half Hardy's and half Eustacia's, and they by no means suggest the consciousness of someone who has begun to enter the true spirit of the natural world by means of the survivals. Yet he certainly means to contrast them with Thomasin's difficult trip across the heath with her baby:

> Yet in spite of all this Thomasin was not sorry that she had started. To her there were not, as to Eustacia, demons in the air, and malice in every bush and bough. The drops which lashed her face were not scorpions, but prosy rain; Egdon in the mass was no monster whatever, but impersonal open ground. Her fears of the place were rational, her dislikes of its worst moods reasonable. At this time it was in her view a windy, wet place, in which a person might experience much discomfort, lose the path without care, and possibly catch cold. (296)

Coming at such length and shortly before the impassioned death of Eustacia, Wildeve, and nearly of Clym, as well as before her marriage to the ultimate pragmatic idealist of them all (a man who can describe the "symbolic" maypole as "a lot of folk going crazy round a stick" [310]), Thomasin's rationality is an important clue to Hardy's thinking at the end of this novel. Survival goes to Thomasin and Venn, somewhat as it does to Cathy and Hareton in *Wuthering Heights*. In this sense, they are really more nearly like the heath (with its genius for survival) than Clym, who although its true child has, like Ruskin, refused to accept survival as either Nature's or his own goal. Venn is an idealist too, loyal and even romantic beyond reason; yet he can both describe the maypole ritual as I have noted above and arrange for it to be staged just beyond Thomasin's front yard, knowing that she will respond to its ancient call as surely as Clym will not.

Yet of course Thomasin and Diggory Venn are no ideal for Hardy. These ruminations on the survival quality of a rational approach to the natural world serve to remind Hardy that, like the anthropologists themselves, Clym has found the "return" plagued with distortions born of his particularly advanced consciousness. Thomasin and Venn are not conscious as he is (albeit that most readers fault Hardy for not properly deepening this "continental" aspect of Clym's disillusionment). And, far more important, Thomasin and Venn do not really make the attempt, have never quite been native in the sense that Clym has. They have no way of knowing that even though Nature will not tolerate the imposition of peculiarly human prejudices—romantic, ethical, mechanistic, and so on—it offers survival (and a lesser contentment) to those who observe that a pragmatic approach to her mysteries is, ordinarily and at least, a safe one.

The end of *The Return of the Native* is as mysterious as the terms of its major problem suggest: the natural world (which of course must *include* man and especially his apparently aberrant self-consciousness) is not rational, even though Thomasin's approach is best for survival. (Her approach is not foolproof, however, for on that night both she and her baby would have drowned had they not met Venn, with his characteristically detailed knowledge.) If Nature is not rationally arranged, at the end of the novel we are far from understanding what mentality a man might need to find himself consonant and at peace with it. This much the novel establishes quite vividly: any such ultimate peace, such ultimate return, need not be a dehumanizing experience. We are not led to believe either that Clym's near absorption by the heath (when his eyesight has failed and he turns furze-cutter) is the true return or that we should share Eustacia's and his mother's shock at what they see as a great social failure. Indeed, we cannot even feel that Clym has become nearly unconscious, although working till numb and sleeping like the dead. All we can say or need to at this point is that we apparently have a new and terribly elusive otium in the offing, a "peace" thoroughly influenced by the striking attempt of anthropologists from at least 1851 on to use the survival as the key to this kingdom.

That contentment and peace are what is sought we have affirmed by the continual testimony of Clym himself and by Hardy's refusal to undercut that goal in any significant way. What is so entirely remarkable about this novel is that Hardy does not immediately begin to erode Clym's conception of a return. He treats almost sarcastically Clym's theories of education, especially the idea that he can lead the natives from "the bucolic to the intellectual life" without offering them the intermediate stage of social advancement (143). Yet he never intimates that the ancient pastoral ideal has been invalidated by whatever modern virus has infected Clym. And this from a man so steeped in Darwin and the evolutionary anthropologists that we might expect him to conclude simply that a nature "red in fang and claw" could offer, to one seeking consonance with it, only savagery.

The status of the allegedly tragic action in *The Return of the Native* is the best clue we have to the continuing influence of the drive toward a pastoral return in this novel. Such action begins with a flurry immediately after Clym has drawn microscopically close the heath in that famous furze-cutting scene. He feels that the very presence of the heath (with its stoical endurance and characteristically untragic qualities) is antithetical to the passionate, incipiently tragic feelings he experiences while setting out on one of the distraught walks that will eventually bring him to his allegedly tragic identity as a kind of Oedipus. We may speculate that all this action toward a tragic identity for Clym is offered—within the phenomenological economy of both Hardy himself and the novel—as a kind of alternative to the pastoral identity which Clym has taken to such an extremity in the furze-cutting scene. There is every reason to believe that Hardy has offered the intense, tragic action as a surge of human dignity, of intense, egoistic identity; it is offered almost as an antidote to the potentially intimidating possibility of Clym's absorption by the heath in a scene where even the savage heath flies take him to be only another natural element. We do not need a long memory to recognize in Clym's approach to the very essence of the heath something from those earlier blurrings and white-outs and implosions so important to *Far From the Madding Crowd*, even if so small a thing as the song he sings maintains the crucial distance from Nature also signaled by Oak's flute on Norcombe Hill.

An explanation along these lines might then go on to claim that Clym attains his true identity—if not, by any stretch of the imagination, his fulfillment—precisely as a tragic and not a pastoral figure. In a very uncomfortable sense, the whole novel vibrates with the tensions between these tragic and pastoral identities. It is not my purpose here to claim that the pastoral thrust of even a frustrated and ambiguous deep return is the only authentic pulse of this novel, and that all the tragic denouement which is its avowed focus fails either to convince us or to allow Clym a significant stature at the end. On the contrary, the very presence of this basic tension between the pastoral and the tragic is in itself the most eloquent testimony imaginable that we are to take with the utmost seriousness the pastoral implications of the title. If the potency I have alleged in the possibility of a return is not there (if I have misread that pastoral aspect of the novel), why does Hardy even need to risk the embarrassment of relating Clym to Oedipus and Christ? The tragic equipment of this novel, however the reader may feel about it, seems to have been an aesthetic necessity in order for Hardy to allow himself as much of the potent and even frightening new pastoral as he did. Having come really close to the strange new humility evoked by this at once newest and oldest heath-nature, Hardy must immediately have Clym straighten up, walk passionately here and there to gather the bits and pieces of information and experience he needs for an apparently unpastoral tragic identity and dignity. Hardy has not affirmed the tragic mode any more than he has rejected or undercut the pastoral. It may be that *The Return of the Native* in its most unique aesthetic purpose makes them a tribute to one another or has created, after the manner of *Far From the Madding Crowd*, another of those intense Hardian pairs, in which we may see how pastoral and tragedy depend on one another in the character of this Janus-like hero.

Three
The Mayor of Casterbridge
and The Woodlanders

Hardy does not again engage the problem of relating tragedy to the return until what Michael Millgate calls his period of "recession" is over and the minor novels of 1880–82 have been published. Of these three (*The Trumpet Major*, 1880; *A Laodicean*, 1881; and *Two on a Tower*, 1882), *A Laodicean* is fundamentally interesting for its relation to Matthew Arnold's definition of modernism as "imaginative reason" and for its intense if awkward concern with the problem of relating the present to the past. Hardy in 1885 was settling in at Max Gate, discovering Roman burials in the very foundation diggings for his new house, relating himself once more to his ancient birthplace of Dorchester, and in general associating the correspondence of man with Nature (the "return" in some sense) with the various aspects of mind or consciousness (imagination, reason, will, senses, and so on) that might be involved in any such return. Arnold says in a passage from the essay "Pagan and Medieval Religious Sentiment":

> The poetry of later paganism lived by the senses and understanding; the poetry of mediaeval Christianity lived by the heart and imagination. But the main element of the modern spirit's life is neither the senses and understanding, nor the heart and imagination; it is the imaginative reason.[1]

The comment is typically symmetrical and committed to a rather unexamined faculty psychology which Hardy intuitively undercuts by having Paula Power in *A Laodicean* refer to it as the view of a "finished writer." Yet the phrase is important to his own manner of relating present to past in that novel and even more so in *Jude the Obscure*, where the isolation of "reason" in Sue Bridehead becomes the paradigm of modernism.

In short, Hardy moves from the question of what constitutes a tragic figure in *The Return of the Native* to nearly the same issue in *The Mayor of Casterbridge*, but always by placing the problems of tragedy in the context of the return, of the correspondence of man to Nature. The two issues were apparently inseparable in his imagination, a fact that has not been sufficiently emphasized by those who regard him as an accomplished tragedian. Although all tragic figures seem inevitably to invoke questions of man's relation to Nature, and that because tragedy must be played against some coherent cosmic scheme of value, no one links tragedy with man's frustrated rediscovery of the true correspondence so insistently as Hardy. In *The Woodlanders* (1887), a similar scenario is played out for Grace Melbury and her frustrated love for the earth god Giles Winterborne. It may well be that for a writer who had never had any theological sense of a cosmic scheme of value, Christian or otherwise, the ancient folk sense that if Nature cohered in ways beyond man's describing, it nonetheless cohered, was both cosmic enough and value enough. If Hardy was able to create a genuinely tragic figure, it perhaps had to be against this natural background—against this problem of the correspondence. And most likely it had also to be in terms of whatever psychological or psychic faculties were paramount in the modern sensibility—were available in contrast to an ancient rustic sensibility that had created its great monuments to the achieved symbiosis in, say, Mai-Dun (Maiden Castle) or Stonehenge.

These are the imaginative categories with which Hardy approaches *The Mayor of Casterbridge*. Most readers agree that with Henchard, Hardy comes closer to creating genuine tragic stature than with Clym or Eustacia, and that with Jude we have tipped over into recognizably modern pathos rather than tragedy. But it may be more nearly correct to say that the very idea of tragedy finally seems to Hardy one of those nets that neither the ancient builders of Stonehenge nor Tess herself would have cast in the first place. Surely after *The Mayor of Casterbridge* not all his reading in Greek drama can save tragedy for the modern world.

Nevertheless, the ontological inspiration that guides this novel may best be described not as a further exploration of Hardy's sense of the tragic hero but as a willingness to probe one kind of being in terms of another kind—not simply synaesthesia or even the mixed categories of metaphysical poetry, but a peculiar experimentalism that, by the end of chapter four, has the reader accepting not only "loaves . . . as flat as toads" (made with Henchard's "growed wheat") but the designation of those loaves as "unprincipled bread": "I've been a wife, and I've been a mother, and I never see such unprincipled bread in Casterbridge as this before." This is the first characteristic of the "new" Henchard that Susan and Elizabeth-Jane encounter on their entry into Casterbridge. And yet it is not unlike the capacity of the old Henchard to unprinciple things, to deny them something of their essence and substitute something of the informing principle of another kind of being. The wife auction has been just such an activity.

It is the "crime" that takes him out of the natural life in the fields and puts him into commercial society. Earlier he had worn "leggings yellow as marigolds, corduroys immaculate as new flax, and a neckerchief like a flower garden." After the wife auction, he enters a world that can make him mayor but can never erase what D. H. Lawrence called the "true correspondence between the material cosmos and the human soul."[2] As John Paterson suggests and as I have shown throughout his first two great pastoral novels, Hardy, like his follower D. H. Lawrence, sought to expand the significance of his characters beyond "the functions of their merely social values and conditions . . . and to make them participants in some larger non-human drama."[3] The very metaphoric texture of Hardy's prose will often suggest not that some human feature, physical or psychological, is "like" some aspect of Nature (as in John Paterson's example of Tess's "peony mouth" or in nearly every metaphor we have examined thus far) but that some larger ontology comprehends both. Hardy intends to expand our understanding of human nature by suggesting that the mainstream of the Victorian novel (with its key image of the web, man in society affecting and affected by the slightest movement of any strand) has led us to forget ancient connections with the nonhuman world.

Thus, the wife auction stands at a symbolic moment in Henchard's life, when he is willing to apply a commercial trope to matters between him and his wife (and between him and his self-image) that are not of that order of being, that are ontologically inappropriate, as, for example, other kinds of violence or even desertion would not have been. The auction signals the triumph of social and commercial signification over the more primitive, even atavistic sources of Henchard's being. Using the commercial trope to carry his feelings, whatever they may be, plunges Henchard out of his native element and into a commercial and social world where the talents of Farfrae will eventually, and with no malice, wear him down and finish him off. His life suggests the danger of allowing a man's social significance to be effectively severed from his nonhuman significance, from the source of his energy in natural forces that are not to be gambled upon in commercial speculation.

To begin the novel with such confusion of ontologies unsettles the "nature," the secure essence, of other things throughout the story. It is almost as though the wife auction in some atavistic way had been blasphemy against the principle that such essences had better not be confused lest all Nature be set askew, decentered so that even names no longer seem to go to the heart of things and begin to lead a vagrant life of their own. To call the bread "unprincipled" is far more than a rustic description intimating that Henchard is unprincipled for having sold the bakers and millers sprouted wheat, or the millers unprincipled for claiming they did not know it had sprouted, or all unprincipled for colluding in the deception (the most unprincipled thing of all). Bread, called symbolic of the transition from Nature to culture by men as different as Claude Lévi-Strauss and Thoreau, has thus been unprincipled as surely as Henchard's wife auction had earlier struck at marriage. We may well remember Thoreau's satire of those who would call yeast the essence of bread and his successive elimination of ingredients in search of a more genuine candidate for the role. Like Hardy, Thoreau was a great seeker of essences; not to know them was, after all, to miss Thoreau's own version of the "true correspondence between the material cosmos and the human soul."

The incident with the bread, the wife auction, and, later, such incidents as Henchard's gambling on the weather are all exquisitely structured to suggest just such confusion. Somehow Susan's initially naive and "meek" belief in the "binding force" of the "transaction" strikes us as morally justified and really no mixing of ontologies at all. Henchard's subsequent pledge to stop drinking for as long as he has already lived (twenty-one years) emphasizes only that his capacity for unprincipling his own life has little to do with his drinking. Liquor may have precipitated the crisis, but within him works the ancient antagonist of the pastoral otium, ambition itself, the aspiring mind. We are once again very much in the presence of Hardy's pastoral *Gestalten*, asking the ancient questions, reexamining the nature of otium, suspecting that it may consist in knowing what things are in their essence and particularly what common being man may share with the "material world."

That Hardy is particularly anxious to see man as anything but a unique mode of being we see upon Henchard's leaving the scene of the crime. Surely there was a part of Hardy that would have relished treating marriage as a mere contract, at least insofar as society forced other emotional and moral aspects of the relationship to conform painfully with that commercial mold. In his fascination with the wife auction (his poring over antique instances of it in county records), it is as though Hardy were saying to society: all right, you covertly regard marriage as a contract and commercial expediency while sanctifying that commercialism as though it were a spiritual thing sanctified by God. Let us bring its commercialism out in the open and, through the hyperbole of the auction, push it to a logical conclusion, or at least to a *reductio ad absurdum*. You will not make its legal and commercial aspect serve its psychological and moral reality, as wise men would; instead, as with Jude, you will allow the legal forms to victimize the psychological reality. So be it. If it is really commercial, let us externalize that essence and epitomize it in the auction. If it is spiritual, let us have no more of this covert commercialism.

The wife auction as a symbol is nicely arranged for the ontological exploration of a social institution as much as it is a complex revelation of Henchard's passing from the roughly georgic and pastoral world to the world of mayors and towns and business. Many of Hardy's symbols are precisely of this borderline variety, poised so that both author and reader may look off into two ontologically different sorts of country.

This mixing of categories is to be seen, then, as a means of gingerly probing the being of things—and certainly as a healthy and creative activity for the author. Within Henchard, however, and without the conscious manipulation that the author can manage for himself, such unprincipling can be tragic. Something of its process may be in the nature of art, but it is a dangerous element in a man's life if he is no artist, and possibly even if he is. When Henchard walks out of the tent, Hardy notes that "the difference between the peacefulness of inferior nature and the wilful hostilities of mankind was very apparent at this place." Yet he immediately remembers that mankind might "some night be innocently sleeping when these quiet objects were raging loud" and includes Henchard's violence and Nature's under the comprehensive ontology of "all terrestrial conditions," which are "intermittent."

That Henchard's hostility has been "wilful" is not sufficient to exclude it from this category. Man's will is no ultimate determinant of ontology for Hardy, and Hardy's motive in this philosophic rumination (really an act of considerable daring) is no less expansive for his view of human nature than, for instance, seeing the sun in Elizabeth-Jane's loosely combed hair as though it were in some mode the same as the sunlight penetrating a hazel copse. There is nothing mystical in either of these perceptions; they are, rather, eloquent proof of Hardy's taste for the immanent reality of both the visual moment in the hazel copse and of a nearly unnameable quality in Elizabeth-Jane. The connection may depend on the most delicate perception of modes of being, but it is not transcendent in any Emersonian or Platonic sense. In some entirely legitimate sense of the word, it is more nearly empirical. As Hardy has said in a note, "In spite of myself I cannot help noticing countenances and tempers in objects of scenery, e.g., trees, hills, houses."[4]

While it is not true that the whole plot of *The Mayor of Casterbridge* consists of the consequences of this auction come back to haunt him, still the novel unfolds a sequence of paradoxes built upon the ontological symbol. The man whom Henchard loves, Farfrae, becomes his commercial rival largely because Henchard, having plunged into the commercial world, will not recognize that it is nonetheless outside his nature. While Henchard deals with a handshake and a "Ye shall hae't," Farfrae writes out contracts and balances books; his talent for romance never impinges on his equal talent for orderly business. He sings nostalgic songs about a Scotland he never particularly wants to see again. He weighs alternatives and is expert in taking into account the feelings of others without really responding to those feelings. In short, he is totally untragic and has been made so in contrast to the self-defeating paradox of Henchard. Farfrae is an uncanny portrait of what might be called, in comparison with the Industrial Revolution, the Managerial Revolution.

Henchard's tragic qualities have been variously described, ranging from a subtle "self-destructive" wish and melancholy need to strip people of their dignity, to a taste for liquor and a simple bad temper that plunges ahead without any long-range sense of consequences. If the wife auction, however, is a clue to the qualities in him that are tragic, we shall need to understand the paradoxes it produces in the subsequent action of the novel. Susan becomes a true wife to a man whose legal wife she can never be. She returns to a Henchard whose legal wife she is but with feelings and a child that in every sense belong to Newson. The auction creates a situation where there can be no further correspondence between social form and emotional content. Henchard, like some of Joseph Conrad's characters, has committed a "crime" which has jolted things out of their customary significations and made us wonder, indeed, whether even names have anything intrinsic to do with what they are supposed to designate in the social and material world.

Especially Elizabeth-Jane sees the world in this seminal disorder as she sits the death watch beside her mother's bed. She is, after all, the victim of so many of these dislocations and dissociations. She hears

> the timepiece in the bedroom ticking frantically against the clock on the stairs [two orderly measures of time and "reality" disagreeing stubbornly with one another]; ticking harder and harder till it seemed to clang like a gong; and all this while the subtle-souled girl asking herself why she was born, why sitting in a room, and blinking at the candle; why things around her had taken the shape they wore in preference to every other possible shape. Why they stared at her so helplessly, as if waiting for the touch of some wand that should release them from terrestrial constraint; what that chaos called consciousness which spun in her at this moment like a top, tended to, and began in. Her eyes fell together; she was awake, yet she was asleep. (135–36)

As Susan dies, she attempts to designate every detail of her funeral (down to the pennies on her dead eyes), to thrust Elizabeth-Jane into Farfrae's care, and in general to control all the details of existence that Elizabeth-Jane feels are about to spin out of their named and accustomed categories.

Yet the world, especially as it seems to exist after Henchard's crime, will not tolerate such management, any more than Elizabeth-Jane's name or the weather at harvest time will. Confronting Elizabeth-Jane with his desire to change and thereby manage her name, Henchard says, " 'Twas I that chose your name, my daughter; your mother wanted it Susan. There, don't forget 'twas I gave you your name!" But if in Hardy's world names are manipulated, essences cannot be, and Henchard has invited the wrath of the nonexistent gods in his bit of hubris.

Elizabeth-Jane, anxious to stop the ontological spinning mentioned earlier, says, "If it is my name I must have it, mustn't I," and Henchard, anxious to disguise the role of his own will in the matter says, "Well, well; usage is everything in these matters." Of course no sooner is the notice to the newspapers dictated than Henchard goes upstairs to find evidence of her name and discovers Susan's letter saying that Elizabeth-Jane is Newson's child. When, after an anguished walk that night, he returns to his newly named daughter, who is no daughter, ironically he finds an Elizabeth-Jane who from this moment on calls him father and nearly becomes his emotional child. This kind of irony concerning the identity of things and people is fundamental to *The Mayor of Casterbridge*.

Henchard creates his own fate by denying "the true correspondence between the material cosmos and the human soul," by cutting himself off from a genius for such symbiosis in the sense of not recognizing the wellspring of his true temperamental power. But he nonetheless dies having disappeared as though "he had sunk into the earth," on the borders of the Ishmaelite Egdon Heath and among the tumuli of the earliest tribes, tombs which look like the breasts of "Diana Multimammia fully extended there." In his death the connection is reaffirmed. Farfrae may interpose harvesting and planting machines between the primordial sower and reaper and their connection with the very soil they turn, but Farfrae has nothing to lose in the way of that true correspondence: his temperament is modulated by rational considerations that Great Mother knows nothing of. She is tempestuous or tranquil in the passionate manner of a Greek god. And in Henchard, Hardy has phenomenologically caught this quality; it is the key to both his stature—as it is Lear's—and his fall. Although Henchard is nevertheless defined symbolically with a return to the multiple breasts of the earth, Hardy is obviously not yet finished with the hero who represents that great struggle between the demands of Farfraeite modern culture and society and those of the true correspondence. In *Tess of the d'Urbervilles*, the pull of both forces intensifies, and Hardy answers with a soul equal to the struggle—indeed, with an absolutely fierce and pagan spirit who can make it back not only to the borders of Egdon, symbolically speaking, but to the pagan altar of Stonehenge itself.

That analysis of *Tess of the d'Urbervilles*, however, requires one more meditation on the return—that great Hardian intersection of themes—this time in *The Woodlanders*, a novel largely frustrated in discovering its own meaning but one nevertheless that Hardy apparently had to write before tragedy itself could be transcended in a new pastoral heroine.

The Woodlanders is a much better novel than its rather automatic repetition of so many familiar Hardian motifs would suggest. A country girl is educated beyond her humble origins so that she misses real pastoral happiness with a local Gabriel Oak, marries a romantically aspiring dilettante who dabbles in modern philosophy, loses him to an aristocratic lady, suffers the death of her young "fruit-god" or "wood-god" (a death due partly to his own punctilious sense of decorum and partly to unjust divorce laws), and finally is rather mysteriously reconciled with her penitent—and still genteel—handsome husband. At first glance this frustrated pastoralism would seem to add little to my earlier discussions of the new pastoralism in the three previous novels. Yet there are peculiarities in *The Woodlanders* that make it necessary to pause before undertaking the culmination of Hardy's pastoralism in *Tess of the d'Urbervilles* and *Jude the Obscure*. Most important, in *The Woodlanders* Hardy presents the conflict in his own mind between various forms of philosophic idealism and his natural phenomenological instincts. Ordinarily, phenomenology and philosophic idealism in its many forms are thought to be nearly opposites.

Hardy may or may not be the philosophical idealist Brennecke claimed he was in 1924.[5] Considering the tremendous warping and waffling any "philosophy" undergoes if it is at all integral to a work of fiction, it seems nearly useless to subject a novelist to these philosophical categories. Yet Hardy is as much to blame for the labeling as Brennecke or subsequent students of Hardy's philosophic origins. Hardy, after all, could be fairly pedantic about these philosophic matters even in the most imaginatively stimulating contexts of *Tess of the d'Urbervilles*.

In *The Woodlanders*, he surely was: Marty South cannot even step over her threshold into the night without Hardy remarking that it was "like the very brink of an absolute void, or the ante-mundane Ginnung-Gap believed in by her Teuton fore-fathers" (15). Marty is the true equal of Giles Winterborne in understanding and identifying with Nature. And, as in the above instance, she is also invariably an entrée to a sense of the pastoral and a sense of antiquity linked as we have come to expect in Hardy. After she has cut her hair in order to supply a wig for Mrs. Charmond (the natural being violated for the entirely artificial), "She dreaded it [looking in the mirror] as much as did her own ancestral goddess the reflection in the pool after the rape of her locks by Loke the Malicious" (20). Again, our sensitivity to her natural vitality, especially as suggested by the hair-cutting incident, is immediately underlined by one of these rather awkward references to her ancient identity among the Teutonic legends. We know from many sources that Hardy had been reading a good deal of Von Hartmann, Schopenhauer, Spinoza, and idealistic philosophy in general at about this time in his life, and there is ample evidence that he had continued his reading in comparative mythology and, obviously, in Teutonic mythology. *The Woodlanders* is full of this insistent underlining of pastoral elements with the archaic identification so characteristic of the comparative method.

Thus, we are entirely prepared for Grace's temporary but passionate rejection of the pseudo-Promethean (306) modernism of Fitzpiers in favor of a "passionate desire for the primitive life," "her revolt for the nonce against social law" (248), and her image of Winterborne as some sort of fertility god from the world of *The Golden Bough*:

> He rose upon her memory as the fruit-god and the wood-god in alternation: sometimes leafy and smeared with green lichen, as she had seen him amongst the sappy boughs of the plantation: sometimes cider-stained and starred with apple-pips, as she had met him on his return from cider making in Blackmoor Vale, with his vats and presses beside him. (335).

In descriptions like this we are very close to D. H. Lawrence without the overt sexual lyricism. The sexuality is of course there, and for other less likely passages of his novels Hardy was severely criticized and even censored. For my purposes, however, it is important to notice that to Grace the pastoral life is also the "primitive life" with all its implications of following the pastoral back to essential man, whatever that might be.

Hardy is often no more certain of what a return to primitive life might mean than is Grace herself. We are constantly made aware that such a return involves many risks and mysteries, all of them somehow pivoting on that phrase "revolt . . . against social law." Grace rebels "for the nonce"— but Hardy is contemplating an essential humanity almost *prior* to social law and certainly prior to the social law of Victorian England. If he moves toward some conception of a culture consonant with Nature, it is not an easy movement that will leave us with jolly rustic fetes about the cider mill and assorted fertility gods and goddesses. The face of true archaism is enigmatic. The escape from "social law" or at least from incredibly artificial social law is initially by way of a certain perspectivism and relativism. The social self must perhaps initially experience a weightlessness and shapeless potentiality. But ultimately, for Hardy, the self must confront the possibility of a "return" to origins. As the modern anthropologist Mircea Eliade says, the primitive mind believes that to know the origin of something is to control it.[6] Thus, he argues, mythology consists largely of origin stories which are narrated and reenacted to gain control over the subject of the myth, however complex that subject may be.

The consciousness which is most comfortably imagined by Hardy is the totally free-floating perspectivist potential. Fitzpiers in the forest "dreamed and mused till his consciousness seemed to occupy the whole space of the woodland round, so little was there of jarring sight or sound to hinder perfect mental unity with the sentiment of the place" (165). His consciousness is the shapeless potentiality that fills available space, that makes its own evanescent reality, skipping from infatuation with Grace to infatuation with Mrs. Charmond, and back to Grace again, tempted only momentarily by a weak pastoralism that suggests he might forego his "philosophic" ambitions "to live in calm contentment here, and instead of going on elaborating new conceptions with infinite pains, to accept quiet domesticity according to oldest and homliest notions" (165). He manages to make even the tough pastoralism that Hardy contemplates—one following back to primordial sympathies—a rosy, washed-out domesticity.

Fitzpiers mouths philosophic catch phrases largely to fill the boredom ("There's only Me and Not Me in the whole world" [55], a peculiarly anti-phenomenological thought) and yet Hardy uses Fitzpiers's most significant philosophic focus to distinguish between two kinds of idealism. Fitzpiers is a Platonic idealist who believes that the world of appearances is a poor and broken reflection of the world of ideas, of Platonic forms. He studies "a fragment of old John South's brain" in order "to carry on simultaneously the study of physiology and transcendental philosophy, the material world and the ideal, so as to discover if possible a point of contact between them" (156). Such an intersection is the most ancient of problems, surely, and one which interests Hardy. But if Hardy is an idealist at all, his idealism has a different emphasis.

Fitzpiers regards the old problem of the relationship between ideal and material with a fine aesthetic languor that reminds one of Eustacia's aesthetic treatment of human emotions and is characteristic of his sentimentalism and romanticism in general. Hardy says that few people could grasp the state of mind in which Fitzpiers returns to his deserted wife, Grace.

It was naturally quite out of his [an observer's] power to divine the singular sentimental revival in Fitzpiers's heart: the fineness of tissue which could take a deep, emotional—*almost also an artistic*—pleasure in being the yearning *inamorato* of a woman he once had deserted would have seemed an absurdity to the young sawyer. (my emphasis, 420)

He even develops a romantic notion that Grace represents the reunion of the material and the ideal.

"I thought, what a lovely creature! The design is for once carried out. Nature has at last recovered her lost union with the Idea. My thoughts ran in that direction because I had been reading the work of a transcendental philosopher last night; and I dare say it was the dose of Idealism that I received from it that made me scarcely able to distinguish between reality and fancy." (154)

Passages of this sort would be enough to convince most readers that Hardy intended a gentle satire of idealism, were it not for the fact that the author himself is clearly preoccupied with his own variety. Describing a profusion of highly competitive life forms in the forest, Hardy says:

Here, as everywhere, the Unfulfilled Intention, which makes life what it is, was as obvious as it could be among the depraved crowds of a city slum. The leaf was deformed, the curve was crippled, the taper was interrupted; the lichen ate the vigor of the stalk, and the ivy slowly strangled to death the promising sapling. (59)

We might suppose that an author well-read in Darwin would simply understand all this ruthless competition among various life forms as natural selection and let it go at that. But there is a fairly good chance that by 1887 Hardy had already read Edward Von Hartmann's *Philosophy of the Unconscious*, published in German in 1868 (Hardy did not read German very well) and translated into English by W. C. Coupland in 1884. It was said that Hardy owned a Coupland edition of 1893, but in view of these allusions to the Unfulfilled Intention in *The Woodlanders*, it seems likely that he had at least become acquainted with it before 1887.[7] In discussing psychic phenomena while working on *The Dynasts* in 1901, Hardy suggests that although the evidence for such manifestations is pitifully incomplete,

> Is not this incompleteness a characteristic of all phenomena, of the universe at large? It often seems to me like a half-expressed, and ill-expressed idea. Do you know Hartmann's Philosophy of the Unconscious? It suggested to me what seems almost like a workable theory of the great problem of the origin of evil,—though this, of course, is not Hartmann's own theory—that there may be a consciousness, infinitely far off, at the other end of the chain of phenomena, always striving to express itself, and always baffled and blundering, just as the spirits seem to be.[8]

He seems to have associated the Unfulfilled Intention with Von Hartmann and ultimately with his own view in *The Dynasts* that blends Schopenhauer's enigmatic Will with the idea that the universe is created and driven by an Unconsciousness slowly evolving toward consciousness (and, implicitly, toward an ethical awareness).

Hardy, then, is also capable of idealistic thoughts in his attitude toward Nature in *The Woodlanders*. It is not that Nature blindly selects the hardiest plant and the most useful variation but that even this seemingly dumb encouragement of mere life, of gross existence and reproduction, is the frustrated, partly revealed shadow of an Intention—not merely life but a purpose for life.

As in so many of Hardy's characters, the principal characteristic of this propagating Idea is unfulfilled intention. And as with Clym Yeobright himself, the most ambitious unfulfilled intention in Hardy may be the quasi-mystical return which in *The Woodlanders* is now not so much toward Nature as toward the Intention that lies mysteriously in and behind Nature. It is in this direction that for Hardy the future of consciousness lies and not in the aesthetic and sentimental indulgence that marks mere subjectivism and perspectivism in Fitzpiers. If Hardy is an idealist in *The Woodlanders*, it is in this sense. He has passed at least spasmodically beyond mere subjectivism; the idealism of his conception of the Unfulfilled Intention is not to be confused with Fitzpiers's indulgent subjectivism.

Fitzpiers may hope to find nature's "lost union with the idea" in an ersatz Shelleyan manner, in an etherialized woman perhaps. Hardy, though he may seek a similar sense of union between the ideal and the real and seek it partly through the same woman Fitzpiers has used, will not idealize her in an enchanted moment between waking and sleep, as Fitzpiers does, but probe phenomenologically her own unadorned imperfection, her own version of unfulfilled intention, and seek in the full phenomenology of this blightedness a further, veiled clue to the ideal. Such is Hardy's toughness and Fitzpiers's flaccidity. Densely intertwined, the two kinds of idealism are nonetheless different.

I must now emphasize that it is largely through the imaginative realization of Grace's unfulfilled intentions, her failure to be what she *should* have been, that Hardy can give us any shadow of the supposed Will behind nature. We know that Hardy is associating Grace's blightedness with the unfulfilled intention he sees elsewhere in Nature by lines such as the following. Grace is watching her husband ride off to—she suspects—his paramour, Mrs. Charmond, and looks closely at the fecund autumnal woods around her, struck by their bounty.

> Acorns cracked under foot, and the burst husks of chestnuts lay exposing their auburn contents as if arranged by anxious sellers in a fruit-market. In all this proud show some kernels were unsound as her own situation, and she wondered if there were one world in the universe where the fruit had no worm, and marriage no sorrow. (245)

Readers familiar with Hardy's pastoral will recognize in the allusion to worms in fruit and sorrow in marriage not metaphor but an ontological lead that inspires him throughout this novel. If *The Woodlanders* is Hardy's comment on idealism, it is more significantly one of his most compelling phenomenologies. The great forest and its inhabitants exist in the same modes, at least until the modern world outside intrudes. Marty South and Giles are perfectly capable of continuing this symbiosis, but, of course, for Hardy the question was not whether the native could remain native but whether the native could return, now carrying the sort of self-consciousness that Clym and Grace acquire in the outside world.

These lines are also an anticipation of Tess's famous comparison of blighted apples and blighted worlds; and when Tess first meets Alec d'Urberville, Hardy feels compelled to give us a short essay about how "In the ill-judged execution of the well-judged plan of things the call seldom produces the comer, the man to love rarely coincides with the hour for loving." He goes on to speculate as to whether subsequent "human progress" will correct this blightedness by "finer intuition" and "a closer interaction of the social machinery than that which now jolts us round and along," thereby suggesting that even though it can still produce rather wordy abstractions, the ontology of blightedness remains a powerful phenomenological strand that draws Hardy on at least through *Tess of the d'Urbervilles* and possibly on to *Jude the Obscure*.

All this theorizing in Hardy often seems no more than useless complaining, but it may help us to understand the lengths to which he will go in attempting to preserve an idealism of "natural" existence despite Nature's blightedness. Hardy is about to offer us a paragraph of Grace's nearly mystical enthusiasm for Winterborne's archaic naturalness:

> He looked and smelt like Autumn's very brother, his face being sun-burnt to wheat-colour, his eyes blue as cornflowers, his sleeves and leggings dyed with fruitstains, his hands clammy with the sweet juice of apples, his hat sprinkled with pips, and everywhere about him that atmosphere of cider which at its first return each season has such an indescribable fascination for those who have been born and bred among the orchards. Her heart rose from its late sadness like a released bough; her senses revelled in the sudden lapse back to Nature unadorned. The consciousness of having to be genteel because of her husband's profession [he is a doctor], the veneer of artificiality which she had acquired at the fashionable schools, were thrown off, and she became the crude country girl of her latent early instincts. (246–47)

Grace's intention is nonetheless blighted and, as I have said, self-consciously related by Hardy to the larger pattern he sees in the blightedness of all nature despite her momentary recovery "like a released bough." Hardy involves Grace and Winterborne in expectations that a recent "reform" in the divorce law will enable them to marry. As we expect, the law has been inadequately reformed:

To hear these two Arcadian innocents talk of imperial law would have made a humane person weep who should have known what a dangerous structure they were building up on their supposed knowledge. They remained in thought, like children in the presence of the incomprehensible. (340)

When Grace allows Winterborne to remain outside his hut for several days while she lives within—and thereby effectively though unwillingly kills the sick man—Hardy has very dubiously shifted responsibility for this failed union as much to society's laws and mores as to Grace's strong "Daphnean instinct" and thereby deprives us of further exploration into Grace's own psychological "blightedness" (359). Winterborne's own punctiliousness is as much to blame as Grace's. During one of the rainy autumn days she waits in the hut, Grace watches the small animals who "knew neither law nor sin" (369). Although Grace would have us believe that Winterborne's death is at least partly the measure of "the purity of his nature, his freedom from the grosser passions [!], his scrupulous delicacy," there is another aspect of Hardy that seems to detect the dishonesty of this entire denouement, to detect a timidity that lies in Hardy's reluctance to explore what his pastoralism and sense of man's aboriginal nature may have to say about knowing "neither law nor sin." This probing he was to do partly in *Jude the Obscure*—creating a public indignation that literally drove him from the novel to poetry and ultimately *The Dynasts*—and more subtly in *Tess of the d'Urbervilles*, where what it means to be intuitively beyond these laws is vividly realized.

The Woodlanders as pastoral is nonetheless as fully committed to the old dichotomy of otium and the aspiring mind as any of Hardy's earlier work. Musing upon the possibility of becoming "welded in with this sylvan life" (141), Fitzpiers speculates that "The secret of happiness lay in limiting the aspirations" (160). His own self-image as a modern Prometheus is meant, again, to produce echoes of the archetypal aspiring mind. Hardy again associates his caricature of modern aspiration with remnants of old families no longer able to aspire in the ancient ways of land and titled influence. Grace's father, having suffered disgrace as a boy for not knowing "Who dragged Whom round the walls of What?" (31) is delighted that he has been able to give his daughter the panache of a fashionable education and that she may wed somebody related to "the long line of the Lords

Baxby of Sherton. You'll feel as if you've stepped into history" (192). This fashionable antiquity has affinities with Fitzpiers's "modern" experiments in chemistry, physiology, and philosophy in that all are subsumed under a romantic, sentimental aestheticism, much as Eustacia's dreams of Paris and the tragedy of a great love are easily conflated in her aestheticism of fine feelings.

The precise nature of this aspiration is not so engaging, however, as the deepening complexity of the otium. The rapprochement with Nature now involves for Hardy at least pursuing an understanding of the intention which is so obviously unfulfilled in plants and animals and man himself. There can be little doubt that in meditating on the qualities in Grace (quite apart from the unnatural law of society) which keep her from the primitive life with her fruit-god, Hardy felt that he might establish some eidetic intuition of the same quality that blights the idea in nature. Such a faith comes close to the very soul of late-nineteenth-century phenomenology. The somewhat generalized implication is that we may glimpse man's essence by insistently imagining the contours of his blight. For Hardy, the blight on Victorian culture is its estrangement from Nature, and these dichotomies of nature and culture and material and ideal are closely related in Hardy's mind by the end of *The Woodlanders*. In fact Fitzpiers's carrying on "simultaneously the study of physiology and transcendental philosophy, the material and the ideal, so as to discover, if possible, a point of contact between them" (156) is a potent clue to Hardy's main formulation of the problem—a problem that is still largely expressed in a fictive rather than baldly philosophical way even in *The Woodlanders*.

Consider that one meeting point of the material and the ideal would be a culture so predicated upon man's natural and archaic identity that no serious discrepancies arise between Nature and culture. More significantly, however, the material and the ideal would "meet" if some feature of the material, natural world could legitimately seem an ideal to human consciousness. Spencerianism had attempted such a reconciliation, but with brutal implications. It is safe to say that Hardy by the conclusion of *The Woodlanders* is vigorously if perhaps somewhat unconsciously seeking an aspect of evolutionism that would be intrinsically and simultaneously "material" and "ideal," a genuine meeting of the two. Any such meeting point of the material and ideal would be tantamout to an expression of essence; it would be an anchor for the floating potentiality that was to be so characteristic of modern consciousness. The "material" world now meant to him, as indeed it may have meant in part to the schoolmen who pondered angels on the head of a pin, a complex array of dimly understood processes rather than the sheer materiality of things. The evolutionary processes, as mysterious as they were and continue to be even to modern biologists, were the material world revealed in its most permanent aspect. If a particular living species or rock structure seemed deceptively permanent, the evolutionary process which had produced it was far more so and lay far closer to the essence of materiality than temporary physical characteristics. Of course Hardy's theory of the Unfulfilled Intention is another form of the interest in a meeting point between the material and the ideal, since the intent is the ideal whose frustration has produced the blighted material nature.

In all this, we may see an especially interesting ontology for consciousness emerging. Despite Hardy's authorial assurances from time to time in *Tess of the d'Urbervilles* that nature is whatever we imagine it to be, there is a contrary current deeply involved with the imaginative power of the fiction—rather than with the author's rhetorical intrusion—suggesting that the free-floating potentiality of consciousness, although it may be our modern condition, is not our future and is not the natural condition of consciousness. Hardy begins to suggest a meeting point of the material and ideal where consciousness is seen to have a natural identity and not merely to vary at random in complete relativism. What this "meeting point" may be we shall see in *Tess*, and almost in *Tess* alone.

It is clear nevertheless that Grace's return has failed not because the divorce law has been badly reformed, not even because both she and Winterborne have been unwilling to violate their delicate rural ethics or because Hardy has been unwilling to contemplate what a "natural" ethics might be, but largely because there is some block in the very consciousness of Grace that will perennially be attracted to its related form in Fitzpiers. The return is never really an alternative for Grace. As with Clym, Hardy finally arranges insurmountable obstacles to it almost as though, given this hero and heroine, he simply cannot imagine any such thing.

This quality of consciousness that has been missing in Clym and Grace is somehow involved with an ultimate pastoral humility, though it would be of the sort that distinguishes at the very least between a "faintly perceptible bend" of the body and a "bowing of the shoulders," between humility and deference. Grace is also a putative native whose experience in the larger world has apparently spoiled her for a return to her fruit-god and to the great symbiotic forests that are the true genius of this novel. At its worst, *The Woodlanders* offers a philosophic pedantry distinct from the satire of this same pedantic quality in Fitzpiers. At its best, however, the moaning giant trees, the blighted older trees on which "huge lobes of fungi grew like lungs" become the Unfulfilled Intention made palpable, the idea dissolved in the felt presence of a tangible nature. It is true that in this woodland nature and in the heath, natural qualities are revealed that hold off the native who would return, and it is true that in the native himself or herself various subtle kinds of ambition make the pastoral rapprochement impossible. Certainly, Hardy is unwilling to compromise his view of Nature so as to make the return more likely. Like Egdon Heath, the great forests are both beckoning and frightening, intimidating, existing in a mode potent beyond even tragedy and the forms of chastened and enriched ego possible to tragedy. Even the idea that Clym and Grace are frustrated in their returns because of some subtle forms of ambition or aspiration has become so delicate as almost to elude the ancient accusation: in one sense, Clym's residual aspiration and vanity is to require an ethical purpose for Nature, for creation.

In no sense would the return be the annihilation of ego and identity; yet it seems to offer an alternate ego that is so strange to these "natives"— especially to the conventional mind of Grace—that we must seek it in Tess, in such peculiar combinations of humility and ego as Tess's baptizing her own baby and breaking the wounded birds' necks. There is a quality in Tess that allows her, we cannot say to return—for she has never left after the manner of Clym to Paris and Grace to her fancy education—but to undergo a prolonged application of modern skepticism and disillusionment from the man she loves, and to emerge unscathed. It is not easy to say what this quality in her may be, but it would seem to involve a peculiar primordial turn of consciousness that nonetheless retains its knowledge of modern skepticism, and to be definitively missing in Clym and Grace. Hardy may have needed to write both *The Return of the Native* and *The Woodlanders* in order to develop the kind of consciousness in a character and in himself that would allow modern versions of the ancient pastoral return and bring Tess to Stonehenge as the pagan truly come home. In the end, of course, it is the ambitious country boy become the famous, disillusioned author and public figure who "returns" without losing what the great and modern world beyond Dorset has shown him.

Four
Tess of the d'Urbervilles

A curious sort of geological metaphor is submerged in the early chapters of *Tess of the d'Urbervilles*, suggesting time or history as though they were geological strata, earlier strata occasionally visible in the present but in any event all strata necessary for a sense of the present. Thus the two interwoven key notes of the opening scene are John's discovery of his noble ancestry, with its resonance of ancestral seats and lead coffins, and the club-walking, with its parade of women dressed in white and carrying a peeled willow wand and flowers. Hardy suggests that the women's club has lost contact with the original sexual and mythic implications of its May festival, or "cerelia," as Hardy says it may be called. It is a rite of sexuality and fertility, as the peeled willow wand suggests, and perhaps of renewed innocence in the participation not only of virgin maidens but of older, experienced women equally dressed in white, women who embody what William Blake might have seen as a kind of achieved innocence. We are continually reminded by Hardy later in the novel that it is just this capacity for perpetual innocence that Tess possesses despite her seduction by Alec. The white clothes confirm what must have been the ancient ceremony's ability to raise its participants to some state of pagan grace, to some notion of renewed innocence consonant with the renewed fertility, the rite itself declaring the paradoxical association of the one with the other. There is, after all, great attention to the "ideal" whiteness of all the costumes despite the actual variety among them, some actually appearing "of a cadaverous tint" upon close examination. The ceremony has been inherited, Hardy reminds us, in a "disguised form."

What we have here is something very like the analysis of Edward Tylor or of Frazer in *The Golden Bough*. A contemporary ceremony is examined as a survival, almost as though it were a living fossil, and much as Hardy examines the great bonfires in *The Return of the Native*. The Catholic Mass? Surely man has eaten the god for eons. The murder of the priest in the grove? We may have lost the meaning, but it can be recovered through an almost geological penetration of the strata which comprise its particular formation and by a comparative mythology which simply aids that penetration. One is reminded again of Eliot's *The Waste Land*, where the ur meanings have been all but erased and discredited.

Hardy apparently means to suggest how unfortunate it is that Tess's club no longer has access to the mythic aspect of its dance and parade. Of course what Hardy has suggested about the club-walking is a common enough maneuver in his work and one that we have seen often in his use of the pastoral mode. One can hardly stroll down a lane in Wessex but it becomes a Roman road, and hills are so often tumuli that one feels himself in an atmosphere resembling the final pages of E. M. Forster's *Howards End,* full of ancient implications, where the whole countryside becomes symbolic of an infinitely stratified sense of place.

If this is Hardy's attitude toward the recovery of a mythic past in the instance of the club-walking, he has also woven it in with the related discovery by John of his ancestral past. Will it similarly be good for John to become the facetious Sir John and for Tess to be thrust into the ill-defined dreams of her parents for some liaison with this imagined wealth and importance? The two events seem to invite comparison and to have been intuitively arranged for just this purpose. Indeed, Hardy immediately raises the whole question of Tess's subsequent relation to her d'Urberville past and whether she should have been—after the name of her first important ancestor—a Pagan in some sense. Has she really come "home" to Stonehenge? The easiest explanation for Hardy's association of these two potential recoveries of the past in the opening pages of the novel is simply that his attitude toward the club-walking (that its mythic importance ought to be recovered) is ultimately the same as that toward Tess's recovery (if not John's) of her past: she is better off with it, and it may offer some clue as to "what Tess might have been." It is inviting to suppose Hardy may have felt that any mind aware of both its history and evolution was wiser, if not happier, and better equipped to deal with the immense indifference of things.

Just as the earlier significances of the club-walking flicker beneath its contemporary surface, so do Tess's earlier stages flash forth occasionally: "Phases of her childhood lurked in her aspect still. As she walked along today, for all her bouncing, handsome womanliness, you could sometimes see her twelfth year in her cheeks, or her ninth sparking from her eyes; and even her fifth would flit over the curves of her mouth now and then" (12).[1] An ordinary enough observation surely, but entirely in keeping with the concern in these early pages for the detectable past not only *in* the present but comprising it in some organically geological sense. Somehow the present, 1880, militates against the stratified past as it is felt by even Tess's mother, who carries a "fast-perishing lumber of superstitions, folk-lore, dialect, and orally transmitted ballads." Joan is contrasted with Tess, whose "trained National teachings and Standard knowledge under an infinitely Revised Code" seem to obscure any such feeling. Not that Joan represents some sort of proper attitude toward the past or that all the "lumber" Tess has lost was really the finest folk tradition. But on the whole the implication seems to be that our consciousness of life is vastly improved if its mode involves this attitude toward man's present. The club-walking ought to be understood for what it was in its ancient implications. Somehow Tess ought to be understood this way as well, though precisely what this means it would at this point in the novel be nearly impossible to say.

Of course Tess resists the recovery of her past, largely because she sees it the way we do, as social climbing and pretension—not in any real sense the recovery of ancestral implications. She examines the fake d'Urberville's face for precisely the "vestiges" or "survivals" (to use the appropriate late-nineteenth-century anthropological terms) that might have been detected in the club-walking: "She had dreamed of an aged and dignified face, the sublimation [a marvelously precise word, given our interest here] of all the d'Urberville lineaments, furrowed with incarnate memories representing in hieroglyphics the centuries of her family's and England's history" (33). And Hardy's attitude at this moment, indeed Tess's attitude is that such hieroglyphics should, if they exist, be read, whatever untoward suggestions they may harbor. "Our names," she says, "are worn away to Durbeyfield," almost suggesting not the weathering of an engraving but the slow geological evolution that erodes landscapes.

It is furthermore no accident that the modern country estate of the bastardized Stokes-d'Urbervilles lies adjacent to the contrastingly "primeval" Chase, "wherein Druidical mistletoe was still found on aged oaks, and where enormous yew trees, not planted by the hand of man, grew as they had grown when they were pollarded for bows" (31). It is characteristically Hardian that the mistletoe is "Druidical." And it is interesting to speculate that he sees his country folk as the result of a more-or-less steady evolution from Druidical culture, Christianity representing an interference with such evolution. It would be Christianity, for instance, that has made the meaning of the Maypole dance inaccessible even to the dancers. Hardy seems to associate the ability to be in touch with primeval, pagan meanings with the ability to be in touch with the emotional, primitive sources of one's own being—so that the buried geological or archaeological or even paleontological metaphors of his work really imply an ideal model of consciousness, aware of the primeval energies that have shaped its outward topography. The intellectual influence in all this would not, of course, be Freud but people such as Lyell, Herbert Spencer, the so-called evolutionary anthropologists, and Darwin. Among those who are generally agreed to have influenced Hardy, Schopenhauer's analysis of Will and its often incredible resemblance to Freud's sense of the unconscious must come first to mind.[2] We need not pursue these speculations here, but for me they provide an invaluable scaffolding toward the understanding of Tess.

The well-known "nature" passage used to describe Tess's walks after her first return home has been used to argue Hardy's affinity with Schopenhauer. But if we read this passage without such preconceptions, it becomes rather more complicated, less Schopenhauerian than has been imagined. The particular passage referred to in *Tess*, "On these lonely hills and dales her quiescent glide was a piece with the elements she moved in" (72), and the following two paragraphs affirm more than that "the world is only a psychological phenomenon." Tess's mistake is that she animates nature with an attitude or mood that is antipathetic to it: she feels she is "guilty" and that nature is "innocent." But, says Hardy, both she and nature are innocent. "She had been made to break an accepted social law, but no law known to the environment in which she found herself such an anomaly." She can in a sense create the world of Nature as a psychological phenomenon, but the passage equally suggests that there is also an irrevocable Nature that her psychological perceptions cannot touch, a Nature that is not susceptible to judgments of guilt and must for want of a better term be called innocent. The implication, as generations of critics have noted, is that ideally Tess should not feel guilty. Immediately before this passage we have met the country zealot who goes around daubing his religious "texes" on every likely barn or stile. Both Tess and Hardy feel his categorical condemnations are "horrible" and should be contrasted with the sun worship that characterized Tess's ancestors:

> The sun, on account of the mist, had a curious sentient, personal look, demanding the masculine pronoun for its adequate expression. His present aspect, coupled with the lack of all human forms in the scene, explained the old-time heliolatries in a moment. One

could feel that a saner religion had never prevailed under the sky. The luminary was a golden-haired, beaming, mild-eyed, God-like creature, gazing down in the vigor and intentness of youth upon an earth that was brimming with interest for him. (73)

Although Hardy's attitude toward Christianity is complicated, here we are meant to see that Christianity's capacity for creating guilt is unfortunate and that the old heliolatry had no such intent—that it must have been in this regard an unusually sane religion. Unlike Hardy's usual conception of deities, the sun-god finds earth "brimming with interest for him."

In short, any ability in Tess to make contact with earlier, more primitive (though not necessarily unconscious) levels of her mind might have diminished her sense of guilt. Her "Druidical" past is associated not primarily with oak forests, mistletoe, and whatever else may be authentically Druidical, but with Stonehenge and the worship of the sun. The final and crushing irony of the novel is that as Tess lies on the altar (a pagan come home), the first constable rises just where the sun should have risen. Thus Tess is given over to the restrictions and punishments of modern society rather than to the sun and all it suggests by this time in the novel. Two senses of the word *victim* are simultaneously established. And the sun does suggest this ideal awareness: consciousness as an evolved, organically ancient thing, possessing as dynamic forces in the present the survivals of the past, much in the sense that Tylor, Darwin, and Frazer had established.

The emphasis early in the novel is on Tess's existence as an essentially natural woman, though she is depressed by social codes of behavior. We are treated to the famous description of Tess reaping a field: "A fieldman is a personality afield; a field-woman is a portion of the field; she has somehow lost her own margin, imbibed the essence of her surrounding, and assimilated herself with it" (74). If Tess has not developed the sort of consciousness I have been discussing, she apparently shares with her sex a *disposition* to discount social convention and to recognize in Nature a force indifferent to it. She had earlier animated Nature with her own guilt feelings, but now she recognizes that despite these feelings "the trees were just as green as before; the birds sang and the sun shown just as clearly now as ever. The familiar surroundings had not darkened because of her grief, nor sickened because of her pain" (77). Hardy furthermore speculates as to whether she would grin at her seduction and child were she freed from the pressure of social convention: "Moreover, alone on a desert island would she have been wretched at what had happened to her? Not greatly." "Most of the misery had been generated by her conventional aspect, and not by her innate sensations" (77). Nature, it seems, is not merely a psychological phenomenon but exists in "true correspondence" with Tess. Nature sustains her, and these manifold references to her naturalness are apparently by way of preparation for the famous christening scene, though at first it is difficult to see how they function toward that end.

What happens in that scene, however, is very revealing of Tess's consciousness. She is ready to take upon herself a responsibility that ordinarily belongs to convention and church organization. It is, in other words, a remarkably spontaneous thing she does, in the sense that while respecting the letter of convention she impressively violates the spirit of it. The ceremony shows how far she really is from being the victim of convention and how close she really is to some sort of ill-defined spontaneous existence. The sign of her naturalness and spontaneity is a willingness to stand responsible for one's own standards, to function, as Nature does, with characteristic self-sufficiency. I think we can only make informed guesses at this point in the novel as to what such a "natural" tendency may mean; but it has something to do with the recognition of Tess as a pagan, a motif which runs throughout the novel and in a sense closes it.

Virtually the last reference to Sorrow the Undesired is as "that bastard gift of shameless Nature who respects not the social law," a line that recapitulates all the basic concerns of these few pages leading up to the christening scene and reviews with new energy some of Grace's musings in Winterborne's hut in *The Woodlanders*. Tess is deeply affected by that social law; but her affinity is for "shameless Nature," or, to put it differently, for the truth of her "innate sensations." In these lines Hardy is not just being indignant with restrictive society. It remains to be seen whether this affinity for Nature is part of the total model of consciousness I have been discussing, but it is certain that Tess begins to recover in a natural way: "The recuperative power which pervaded organic nature was surely not denied to maidenhead alone" (84). When a "particularly fine spring came round," "it moved her, as it moved the wild animals, and made her passionate to go" (84). Oddly enough, the last paragraph before "Phase the Third—The Rally" indicates that her now natural recovery is equally in the direction of her ancestors and their country. The parallel is between the natural resurgence of her "invincible instinct toward self-delight" and the potential recovery of her d'Urberville past. These two recoveries are, at least in the implications of this paragraph, running side by side, as though they were analogous to one another or at least had something to do with one another that Hardy did not fully understand.

Tess looks forward to entering d'Urberville country, almost as though recovering some vague sense of her d'Urberville past will be simultaneously drawing closer to her "natural" identity and as though both of these accomplishments were necessary for the truly "pagan" Tess. "All the while she wondered if any strange good thing might come of her being in her ancestral land; and some spirit rose within her as the sap in the twigs" (85). The syntax itself couples and implicitly relates the recovery of the ancestral past and the natural identity; the one seems to touch off what Hardy can only express in the utterly natural flow of sap. We are tempted to read the phrase "strange good thing" as entirely ironical in view of what happens to Tess in the land of her ancestors. But there really is no irony in this paragraph. The phrase does not simply, as dramatic irony, look forward to its opposite. There is a good chance that the land of her ancestors does hold some "strange good thing," and that Tess's increasing awareness of her natural identity will improve that chance. Hardy has said, after all, that "But for the world's opinion those experiences would have been simply a liberal education" (84).

Never having been in this country, she nonetheless "felt akin to the landscape" and finds in the distance the location of her ancestral tombs, her "useless ancestors" (86). "She had no admiration for them now; she almost hated them for the dance they had led her; not a thing of all that had been theirs did she retain but the seal and the spoon" (86). The irony is surely obvious. She inherits far more than the seal and the spoon. Hardy strongly suggests that her ancestors had been crudely misused in John's mercenary quest for kin and that Tess is indeed a d'Urberville. Seeking to use the d'Urbervilles as her family had suggested, it is poetic justice that what Tess gets is a fake ancestor rather than something of the old frightening vitality and authority.

As she plunges into the vale of Talbothays, Tess chants a Christian canticle that to Hardy, however, sounds more like a pagan song of joy: "and probably the half-unconscious rapsody was a Fetichistic utterance in a Monotheistic setting; women whose chief companions are the forms and forces of outdoor nature retain in their souls far more of the pagan fantasy of their remote forefathers than of the systematized religion taught their race at later date" (88). Again we are invited to see Tess in her natural capacity, and this familiar motif is again associated with the return to the land of her ancestors. Christianity is seen to be a thin overlay on an essentially pagan appreciation of natural "forms and forces." The very posts of the dairy barn are presented almost as a fetish, suggesting an apprehension of death and oblivion that can compete with Christian ideas: "wooden posts rubbed to a glossy smoothness by the flanks of infinite cows and calves of bygone years, now passed to an oblivion almost inconceivable in its profundity" (89). This is quite a remarkable phrase and one that suggests this "profundity" is available to a rather un-Christian sensibility. Even the landscape of Talbothays suggests to Hardy those geological ontologies which blend so readily into paleontological ones: "Thus they all worked on, encompassed by the vast flat mead which extended to either slope of the valley—a level landscape compounded of old landscapes long forgotten, and, no doubt, differing in character very greatly from the landscape they composed now" (92). This image can stand quite powerfully for the state of mind Hardy sees in Tess—and, I might add, for the controlling phenomenology with which Hardy approaches this whole novel. What he wants to cultivate in Tess and the reader is a sense of the role of those old landscapes in the present one. The precise mode of their participation in the reality of the present is one of the great late-Victorian issues that crossed the boundaries of a dozen disciplines.

There is every reason to believe that the consciousness of Angel Clare as it is first and brilliantly presented to us is meant to be a contrast to the potential in Tess that is suggested by the landscape just mentioned—that when he thinks, "What a fresh and virginal daughter of Nature that milk-maid is!" (102), he is far from appreciating the relation of Tess to Nature that I have been discussing in this chapter and is using the word "virginal" in a cruelly different sense from the ones established in the novel. Tess is not only close to Nature, but her virginity ideally comprehends the seduction and child and is continually renewed by her undiminished capacity for innocence. All this is remarkably like cyclical Nature renewing itself and is suggested by the May ceremony that began the novel. Unfortunately, Angel means something remarkably conventional by his "virginal" and cannot begin to comprehend the larger and more powerful sense of the word.

On the whole, his psychology as it is presented to us in chapter 18 runs counter to the evolutionism of Hardy's landscapes and of his landscape ontology. Clare regards his religion not as an evolving process somehow to be contained in the mind in the way Hardy views the landscape, "compounded of old landscapes long forgotten," but rather to be ruthlessly pruned of what now seems useless: "an untenable redemptive theolatry" (97). His attitude is not in the direction of the tolerant evolutionary understanding of the landscape image: "My whole instinct in matters of religion is toward reconstruction; to quote your favorite Epistle to the Hebrews, 'the removing of those things that are shaken, as of things that are made, that those things which cannot be shaken may remain.'" I suspect that the metaphor of constructing, or building, or in general *making* religion is uncongenial to Hardy. Angel's cold application of intellect to the evolved body of religion makes it seem too easy to "reconstruct," to subtract and demolish, as though one were working with a badly constructed building. (Hardy's knowledge of architecture moved far beyond any such rough-and-ready notions.) We may count Hardy among those who did not feel it likely or possible that a wholesome ethics could simply be abstracted from "an untenable redemptive theolatry." Whatever else his attitude toward the supernaturalism of Christianity, it was incredibly respectful, even secularly reverent at times. What Tess could have done with her Christianity without the impact of Angel's arguments may be hard to describe, but it would certainly have been blended with the forms and forces of nature in an unmanipulative way.

Although Angel is making "close acquaintance with phenomena which he had before known but darkly—the seasons in their moods, morning and evening, night and noon, winds in their different tempers, trees, waters and mists, shades and silences, and the voices of inanimate things" (101), he is still very much an idealist of Nature and speaks to Tess, even if casually, of "pastoral life in ancient Greece" (106). It is a deceptively ethereal remark by Tess about how "souls can be made to go outside our bodies" that first attracts him to her, whereas the reader may be forgiven for thinking that Tess is after all something of an expert about souls that are inseparable from the body. Angel creates a number of illusions about Tess, foremost of which is his notion that she is a child of his Nature rather than of hers and Hardy's. Nature comes under close examination in these few pages of the novel (102–5), and interestingly enough it is once more coupled with the problem of Tess's inheritance. Several of the most difficult nature passages in the novel are followed immediately by a rather complex revelation of Tess's questioning whether she ought to reveal to Angel her d'Urberville past, this past which she at times so abruptly dismisses as useless.

In one such passage Tess projects a solipsistic attitude onto Nature but seems nonetheless ripe for a consciousness that understands how object reaches out to subject and how the distinction between inanimate and animate blurs in a correspondence she cannot yet grasp:

> It was a typical summer evening in June, the atmosphere being in such delicate equilibrium and so transmissive that inanimate objects seemed endowed with two or three senses, if not five. There was no distinction between the near and the far, and an auditor felt close to everything within the horizon. The soundlessness impressed her as a positive entity rather than as the mere negation of noise. It was broken by the strumming of strings. (103)

So thoroughly is nature here shaped by the mind of the sensor that what is clearly a sensual preoccupation on her part turns the notes of Angel's distant harp into his body itself: "They [the sounds] had never appealed to her as now, when they wandered in the still air with a stark quality like that of nudity" (104). What is so remarkable about these few pages in the novel, however, is not this passage alone but the fact that it is followed by a famous and apparently contradictory passage, which I shall quote in full despite its notoriety:

> The outskirt of the garden in which Tess found herself had been left uncultivated for some years, and was now damp and rank with juicy grass which sent up mists of pollen at a touch; and with tall blooming weeds emitting offensive smells—weeds whose red and yellow and purple hues formed a polychrome as dazzling as that of cultivated flowers. She went stealthily as a cat through this profusion of growth, gathering cuckoo-spittle on her skirts, cracking snails that were underfoot, staining her hands with thistle-milk and slug-slime, and rubbing off upon her naked arms sticky blights which, though snow-white on the apple-tree trunks, made madder stains on her skin; thus she drew quite near to Clare, still unobserved of him. (104)

This is one of the best passages Hardy ever wrote, not only for what it is but for its strategic use at precisely this point in the novel. Our senses come alive to the sticky objectionableness of Nature in this decaying yet fecund garden. Whatever symbolism may be suggested by the garden (and readers have had a feast of meanings almost since the moment the novel was published), we are clearly made to smell, touch, see, and generally feel. Who can say with what sense we apprehend snails cracked underfoot, or mists of rank pollen hanging in the air, or the deceptiveness of such colors in weeds, or of "sticky blights" which are nonetheless snow white on the tree? One thinks of the garden in "Rapaccini's Daughter."

More symbolically, as has sometimes been suggested, this is a distinctly Hardian Garden of Eden: nature is untended by any God, and this Angel is certainly no God's messenger. We have, rather, Darwin's "tangled bank," though such an emphasis is really undeveloped because of another purpose in hand. Hardy's point is that *this* is what really lies before Tess, though she cannot see it. Her mind transforms the scene into something like the first passage I quoted. She "was conscious of neither space nor time" (104). Her soul passes out of her body as she has suggested it could while gazing at stars: "She undulated upon the thin notes of the second-hand harp." Even the extraordinarily material pollen "seemed to be his notes visible," the clammy dampness "the weeping of the garden's sensibility" (104). One notes the gratuitous phrase "second-hand" and concludes that along with other evidence this constitutes a perhaps critical emphasis on the difference between "reality" and Tess's at-this-moment transcendent sensibility. The garden is incredibly fecund and sensuous, in keeping with her apprehension of his harp notes as nudity itself, but it is also deceptive, as is her whole transcendent state of mind in the passage.

Hardy's emphasis on what is objectively *there* is meant as a kind of dramatic irony, even a warning about the nature of the relationship developing between Angel and Tess. Angel's talent for bringing out the transcendent quality in Tess runs counter to a rather different relationship with Nature that is equally a possibility for her, a relationship suggested by her sense of having come "home" to Stonehenge, by her being a very old creature rather than, as she says, a new one: "The insight afforded in Clare's character suggested to her that it was largely owing to her supposed untraditional newness that she had won interest in his eyes" (109). This remark is the beginning of one of the most phenomenologically basic issues of the whole novel: the ontological differences between old and new. Thus the long discussion in these few pages about Clare's distaste for old families (108) and Tess's refusal of his offer to teach her history: "Because what's the use of learning that I am one of a long row only—finding that there is set down in some old book someone just like me, and to know that I shall only act her part; making me sad, that's all. The best is not to remember that your nature and your past doings have been just like thousands' and thousands', and that your coming life and doing'll be like thousands' and thousands'" (107).

The awareness of the past that Hardy has suggested through the landscape image discussed above (and, of course, through manifold other means since the first page of the novel) leads not at all to the conclusions Tess has reached about history. Ironically, just a moment after she has thus rejected the past she enhances her resemblance to Job by saying that while she does not want historical knowledge, she "shouldn't mind learning why—why the sun do shine on the just and the unjust alike" (107). Hardy would presumably reject Tess's "long row" metaphor in favor of something like the geological or paleontological one. Even Tess is momentarily persuaded that she ought to mention her forebears to a gentleman like Angel, to show "that she was no spurious d'Urberville, compounded of money and ambition like those at Tantridge, but true d'Urberville to the bone" (108).

Angel's taste, then, is for the "new" man or woman. Witness his zest for the lad named Matt who never heard he had a surname and supposed this was so because his folks hadn't been established long enough. "'Ah! you're the very boy I want!' says Mr. Clare, jumping up and shaking hands wi'en; 'I've great hopes of you'; and gave him half-a-crown" (108). Matt's namelessness is another kind of nudity, if not some kind of deracination. Tess responds wittily on hearing this report of Clare, thinking that her family was so "unusually old as almost to have gone round the circle and become a new one" (108). But it is not "untraditional newness" that Hardy wants, even if Clare does. We can seek Hardy's values by speculating, as I have done, on what the opposite of this newness would be. It would not be Tess's view of history; Hardy sets up that innocent explanation to remind us of Tess's sense that her inheritance is "useless." Even she, however, does not really believe this, and we ought to observe that it is probably as useless as the awareness of those old landscapes contained in the new, or as the knowledge of phylogeny in general, or the Victorian theory that ontogeny recapitulates phylogeny.

It is paradoxically Tess's antiquity that allows her to think and feel what "might almost have been called those [feelings] of the age—the ache of modernism" (105). Significantly, then, it is Angel's music which can "raise up dreams" and "drive all such horrid fancies away" (105). Again, Angel's influence is seen to be antithetical to some awareness that Hardy both fears and values in Tess.

The descriptions of early mornings at the dairy reinforce my feeling that Angel makes of Tess something that she simply is not. "The spectral, half-compounded, aqueous light which pervaded the open mead, impressed them with a feeling of isolation, as if they were Adam and Eve" (110). How much ink has been spilled developing the Edenic implications of this passage, when it should be obvious that Tess is a profoundly experienced creature despite Angel's taste for "newness." He might like to be dealing with an Eve and she with an Adam, but Tess has just been presented to us as one who feels the ache of modernism, an anxiety that presumably depends on some innate sense of the past if not positively of a historical sense. When "the mixed, singular gloom in which they walked" (110) suggests to him the Resurrection hour, Hardy remarks that "he little thought that the Magdalen might be at his side" (110). This reference to Tess's "sin," however, is the least of the ironies present in the whole scene. To observe that this supposed Eve has already fallen suggests the first irony. Another is reached by remembering that despite her fall Tess has a marvelous capacity for innocence and still may be seen as a special kind of Eve. Yet a third level is available to us, however, and this irony involves realizing that Tess is deliberately being *made* untraditional, in any meaningful sense, by Clare himself. Certainly he calls her Artemis and Demeter (111), but far from connecting her genuinely with any traditions, this identification serves only to empty her of any personal identity in favor of a "visionary essence of woman." Tess's answer is the perfectly corrective "Call me Tess," although as a rule she submits to this attempt at transforming a human being into an abstract and transcendent principle. It is almost as though Clare, having lost any belief in the transcendence of his religion, has tried to relocate such transcendence in Tess. If his Christianity has lost its innocence, Tess will be made to resurrect the old feelings.

To say that Tess cannot endure this burden because she has a secret sin is to miss the whole point. No woman, much less Tess, could ultimately have borne it. It is fitting that such ethereal touches as Tess looking "ghostly, as if she were merely a soul at large" (110) and the dew touching her eyelashes as though it were seed pearls, come to an appropriate end not only in the sun that shows her to be a "dazzlingly fair dairymaid only" (111) but in the farmer's practical admonitions to the dairymaid who will not wash her hands and in the "horrible scrape" that means the breakfast table has been pulled into place (111–12).

There seems always the possibility that Angel will come down to earth. Tess is not entirely ethereal to him: "How very lovable her face was to him. Yet there was nothing ethereal about it; all was real vitality, real warmth, real incarnation" (127). We need to keep the word "incarnation" in mind as we observe in the next chapter Sue Bridehead's talent for uncarnating everything. Nonetheless we stumble over the word, just as we do over his speculation immediately following this that her mouth and teeth more than anyone's he had ever seen fulfilled "the old Elizabethan simile of roses filled with snow." He is aware that "they were not perfect. And it was the touch of the imperfect upon the would-be perfect that gave the sweetness, because it was that which gave the humanity" (127). If only his faith in her humanity did not require such indirect affirmation!

That his love for Tess is inextricably bound up in his changing attitude toward life at the dairy there can be no doubt. Hardy describes what Angel's father would have thought: "To the aesthetic, sensuous, pagan pleasure in natural life and lush womanhood which his son Angel had lately been experiencing in Var Vale, his temper would have been antipathetic in a high degree." Hardy makes a tentative connection between this life and what might widely have been "if Greece had been the source of the religion of modern civilization, and not Palestine" (133). When Angel visits his parents to prepare them for news of Tess, he is struck by the narrowness of his brothers' views of life. Though for strategic purposes Angel emphasizes Tess's orthodoxy of religion to his parents, Hardy remarks that such convention is "rather automatic" in Tess and, except for the desire to emphasize this orthodoxy to his parents, Angel "had been prone to slight [it] when observing it practiced by her and the other milk-maids, because of its obvious unreality amid beliefs essentially naturalistic" (139).

We must add to these observations a rather peculiar comment by Angel before he has learned of Tess's ancestry. He and his father are discussing his father's attempt to reform Alec d'Urberville, and old Mr. Clare remarks at Angel's apparent interest in the ancient d'Urberville family: "But it is odd to hear you express interest in old families. I thought you set less store by them even than I." Angel replies: "'You misapprehend me, father; you often do' said Angel with a little impatience. 'Politically I am sceptical as to the virtue of their being old. Some of the wise even among themselves "exclaim against their succession," as Hamlet puts it; but lyrically, dramatically, and even historically, I am tenderly attached to them'" (140). Once again Tess's natural tendencies and the d'Urberville ancestry are brought together in the text, at this point especially significantly because Tess has not yet told Angel of her family. And more particularly, we wonder just what Angel means by "lyrically, dramatically, and even historically." That he is in some sense as attracted to her ancestry as he is to her newness we shall come to see.

Returning to the vale of naturalness and fertility, that "green trough of sappiness," Angel "with a sense of luxury recognized his power of viewing life here from its inner side, in a way that had been quite foreign to him in his student-days; and much as he loved his parents, he could not help being aware that to come here, as now, after an experience of home-life affected him like throwing off splints and bandages" (142). If he still tends to abstract Tess into something foreign to her nature, he has also been much affected to the contrary and is much under the influence of the vale and of Tess. Still, when he sees in a terribly sensuous moment after his return "the red interior of her mouth as if it had been a snake's" (143), Angel cannot accept the sexual details of her waking body for what they are. Hardy, representing Angel's point of view, says: "It was a moment when a woman's soul is more incarnate than at any other time; when the most spiritual beauty bespeaks itself flesh; and sex takes the outside place in the presentation" (143). One cannot resist imagining how D. H. Lawrence would have written the same paragraph. It is amazing how in so sensuous a moment sex nevertheless must be decorously ushered in; the language is peculiar, even if it is partly Hardy's own: "incarnate," "bespeaks itself flesh." Are we speaking of a country girl coming downstairs after a nap and stretching herself sensuously on a hot day, or the incarnation of Christ? Angel still sees Tess as something of a sexual threat (as in the snake's mouth image), but primarily as a threat to his immaculate etherealizing process whereby the sensuous and emotional reality of Tess is made the abstract essence of a mythologized nature.

"He himself knew that, in reality, the confused beliefs which she held, apparently imbibed in childhood, were, if anything, Tractarian as to phraseology, and Pantheistic as to essence" (145). Angel's ideal of pantheism, however, is better expressed a few pages later in the novel:

> All the girls drew onward to the spot where the cows were grazing in the farther mead, the bevy advancing with the bold grace of wild animals—the reckless unchastened motion of women accustomed to unlimited space—in which they abandoned themselves to the air as a swimmer to the wave. It seemed natural enough to him now that Tess was again in sight to choose a mate from unconstrained Nature, and not from the abodes of Art. (147)

We are to read "unconstrained Nature" with some degree of irony. Angel does not, after all, have any idea of what may be suggested by either word of the phrase; he laughs at her suggestion that she is experienced and compares her to a flower "that opened this morning for the first time" (149–50). The comparison of Tess and her milkmaid friends to "wild animals," coupled with the implications of "abandoned," seems ominously consistent with the murder near the end of the novel. In any event, Angel's dichotomy of Nature and Art indicates clearly the category into which he is forcing Tess: she is totally uncontrived, devoid of any attention to pose or effect. So much she may be, but how constrictive of her "natural" identity is this fundamental contrast with Art? And how is such a category to acknowledge her persistently intimated d'Urberville inheritance?

When Tess and Angel deliver the milk to the railway station, they pass "an old manor house of Caroline date" (157), which Angel tells her was one of the seats of the ancient d'Urberville family. Thus begins an intensification of references that have already been frequent to her "inheritance." Angel's interest in old families, even before Tess tells him about her ancestry, is strange for one so dedicated to the new. After her revelation of d'Urberville blood, his behavior, in view of his taste for newness in her, is even more remarkable. He even contrives to spend their wedding night in a d'Urberville house, thus allowing Hardy to cast the events of those few days against the melodramatic presence of the two d'Urberville women whose portraits cannot be removed from the old manor. No doubt these two portraits and the reiterated story of the d'Urberville coach constitute (along with many other details) a kind of Gothic curse on the family, a "ballad" element that is not skillfully handled or very meaningful. Critics have often said so. Yet no one has adequately explained why the d'Urberville material is so pervasive and so often brought into pregnant if not readily comprehensible association with other important motifs. For example, the same few paragraphs which contain Angel's reference to the old manor offer a brilliant description of the modern world in the image of the train as some reluctant creature extending its "feelers" into the primeval countryside and withdrawing, "as if what it touched had been uncongenial." When the light of the engine illuminates Tess, "No object could have looked more foreign to the gleaming cranks and wheels than this unsophisticated girl, with the round, bare arms, the rainy face and hair, the suspended attitude of a friendly leopard at pause, the print gown of no date or fashion, and the cotton bonnet drooping on her brow" (157). Shortly before this moment Angel says, "There is something very sad in the extinction of a family of renown, even if it was a fierce, domineering feudal renown." There is a connection between these identifications.

Tess is indeed fierce—almost, I would suggest, characteristically fierce. She has the capacity of a leopard to kill with natural instinct and even composure. Her love for Angel is fierce, even if forbearance is its outward mode; her loyalty to him is fierce, despite his abandonment of her. It is almost as though in calling Tess natural, Hardy is insisting that we give a distinctly Darwinian flavor to that word, though we may, I think, eliminate Herbert Spencer. As David Lodge has suggested, the characteristics of that garden in which Tess listens raptly to Angel's harp may be attributable to Tess herself.[3] Playing on the "madder stains" in that passage, he rightly concludes (even if "madder" is also a color) that Tess is consonant with the "unconstrained nature" of the garden and that "the force of this connection between Tess and the natural world is to suggest the 'mad,' passionate, nonethical quality of her sensibility." If she moves "stealthily as a cat" through this garden, it may be as the leopard rather than the common household tabby: not that she is about to prey on Angel, but certainly in the sense of her enormous capacity for passionate reaction. Such has been the reputation of the d'Urberville family, even if it had, as Angel suggests, once manifested itself as crass "self-seeking" (159). All the readily apparent differences between the old d'Urbervilles and Tess begin to pale when we recognize a certain unconstrained naturalness in both. Its results in the d'Urbervilles are none too pleasant, but then Hardy is bound in this novel to present a potent antidote to Angel's view of naturalness—one might almost say his myth of naturalness.

David J. DeLaura's view of Angel seems correct: that he is associated with Matthew Arnold and is one "whose sin, like that of the later Arnold, is precisely his imperfect modernism, his slavery in the ethical sphere to 'custom and conventionality.'"[4] DeLaura rightly sees that "for Hardy, Arnold had fatally compromised himself in the seventies by his mediating theological position, metaphysically agnostic but emotionally and morally traditional and 'Christian.'" What Hardy wants is "a greater honesty in confronting (to use Arnold's own youthful phrase) 'the modern situation in its true *blankness* and *barrenness*, and *poetrylessness.*'" To do this Hardy requires that a life be made which does not rely on "comforting theistic palliatives" of the sort which Angel locates in his myth of Tess's naturalness. He is, indeed, almost Wordsworthian in what he expects to derive in the way of values from Tess's natural origins. Those ethics which he expects to separate from the background of "redemptive theolatry" represent less Hebraism than a kind of loosely conceived Hellenism and a "culture" which he proudly cultivates apart from the formal theological basis it has in his two brothers. Why else has Hardy given us the detailed background of old Mr. Clare's refusal to educate Angel at Oxford and Angel's reaction to this?

Yet Angel's carefully dissociated "culture" allows him nonetheless to apply to Tess's revelation the most utterly, hopelessly bourgeois double standard. His Hellenism and his culture are ashes when compared with the natural depths from which Tess now draws her fidelity and determination to survive. Angel, in short, is deliberately set up as a possible answer to the ache of modernism, and he fails utterly, whatever combination of intellectual positions of the seventies and eighties he may be seen to represent. DeLaura interestingly concludes that the source of value Hardy finally offers is "the simple endorsement (predictive of Lawrence) of freer relations between men and women unhampered by the stifling and unnatural standards of a dying civilization": "Hardy's major ethical contrast, pervasive in *Tess* and central in *Jude*, is a simple one between an unspecified 'Nature,' evidently as the norm of some other genuine and personal ethical code, and 'Civilization,' identified with social law, convention, and in the last analysis the moral and intellectual constraints of Christianity." DeLaura thinks this feeling for Nature in Hardy is disguised sentimentalism and calls it "Wordsworthian."

I have been arguing, on the contrary, that it is far from an undeveloped idea, is entirely unsentimental, and is at the roots of Tess's paganism. Culture and its rationalism are a veneer, as Hardy often shows us. But there are seemingly two kinds of culture: the sort Angel proudly cultivates and the kind that is closer to a modern anthropologist's definition. Tess is involved in her own culture and not simply in some direct, palpable contact with Nature. One remembers in this connection Dorothy Van Ghent's speculations about the importance of sheer "earth" in this novel and the role of the folk culture relative to that earth.[5] Her conclusion that Tess springs from the "instinctivism," "fatalism," and "magic" common to that culture would seem to be in conflict, however, with the often-mentioned evidence that Hardy wanted to make Tess an aristocrat (albeit perhaps an aristocratic leopard), a true d'Urberville. Especially when Van Ghent sees these "folk" as "the earth's pseudopodia, another fauna" and emphasizes their humility before chance, calling it "what was to be" ("the folk's humble presumption of order in the rule of mishap"), do we wonder whether Hardy's desire to relate Tess to this elemental "culture," and not solely to Nature as DeLaura supposes, is consistent with the implication that she may be a true d'Urberville.

We may well consider in our understanding of *Tess*—and of *The Woodlanders* and its concern with the unfulfilled intention—one of the entries in Hardy's autobiography: "New Year's thought. A perception of the FAIL-URE OF THINGS to be what they are meant to be, lends them, in place of the intended interest, a new and greater interest of an unintended kind."[6] This new and greater interest emerges when, having thrown conceptual nets and intentions over, say, a character, an author allows the phenomenological instinct to prevail and the character begins to go his own way. No genuine "failure" is involved, of course, but rather—and particularly for Hardy—a striking success. Tess, meant by circumstance to be a daughter of the folk culture, will not be another "fauna." Her very consciousness partakes of the rise and fall of families, ceremonies, innocence, and experience. The evolutionary consciousness which was so vital a part of the late-nineteenth-century sensibility did not look at the "old landscapes" inherent in the present, or at fossils come to light in some dig, as dead and mere curiosities. Such fossil material was, as I have argued earlier, more often seen in current, living society or mind as survivals which, under the analysis of Tylor, Frazer, or even Freud, were seen positively to *help* explain the enigmatic configuration of the present.

There is a generous suppleness in the thinking of many Victorians (not the least of them George Eliot) which allows them to make analogies between old landscapes, fossils, cultural survivals (the "cerelia" which begins *Tess*, and, in the case of Tess certainly, family histories. In Tess the mode of existence of this family history is like that of the old landscapes or of the mumming in *The Return of the Native*. Thus, far from there being a real conflict in the reader's tripartite identification of Tess as a child of nature, of the folk culture, and of the long d'Urberville inheritance, to Hardy's way of thinking the d'Urberville psychic inheritance was itself subject to great and natural evolutionary forces that make it part of Tess's consciousness as much, and in the same way, as the old landscapes are part of Var Vale. Tess's aristocratic family sinks back into a soil of folk culture somewhat in the same sense that there is always a fundamental "ground" from which any number of possible landscapes may evolve. But this ground (we may even elicit here some of the connotations that word has in Gestalt psychology) is always altered by the noble families that have apparently sunk back into it. (Tess is told of many "vestiges" in the debased names of milkmaids and village lads.) And of course the process is being permanently altered if not destroyed by the gradual loss of true folk culture. The cities expand; folk leave the land never to return.

The main point is that Hardy's continual association of Tess's naturalness with her d'Urberville inheritance betrays a hidden but potent bias: to be natural is somehow *like* the violent, self-sufficient, proud d'Urberville family—and very little like Angel's sense of Nature. Furthermore, the "natural" d'Urberville quality in Tess is hers not simply as part of a "long row," but as the old landscapes are part of the presently tranquil Var Vale. Hardy, like many late Victorians, was beginning to be especially sensitive to the record of violence and upheaval that lay buried, but still armed, in the rocks, in innocent ceremonies, in the mind itself. The strata were not only telling an old story but revealing a present process.

It would appear, then, that one of the keys to understanding Tess lies precisely in Hardy's understanding of this crucial late-Victorian view of the relation between past and present. We begin, I think, to appreciate its full flavor by realizing that there are even implications for historiography in these early anthropologists—especially in Frazer and Tylor. Henceforth it will be very difficult for historians to write without borrowing some late-Victorian evolutionary ideas about culture, ideas that come mainly from the evolutionary anthropologists.

For Hardy, it is obviously Darwin who is crucial in these matters. Yet the details of Hardy's vivid reaction to Darwin have been largely a mystery for generations of critics. That Hardy emphasized the evolutionary connections among all life (the relatedness of man and "lower" forms) above the infamous "survival of the fittest" is a point insufficiently emphasized by those who discuss him. It was made some fifteen years ago in an article by Elliot B. Gose, Jr.[7] Gose quotes the crucial passage from Hardy's notebook: "The discovery of the law of evolution which revealed that all organic creations are of one family, shifted the center of altruism from humanity to the whole conscious world collectively." Equally important is Hardy's note written before he began *Tess*: "Altriusm, or the Golden Rule, or whatever 'Love your Neighbor as Yourself' may be called, will ultimately be brought about I think by the pain we see in others reacting on ourselves, as if we and they were a part of one body. Mankind, in fact, may be and possibly will be viewed as members of one corporeal frame."[8] Whether Comte or Schopenhauer is more nearly reflected here, the evolutionary bias is toward creative evolution, and toward seeing Darwin's impact less in Spencerian terms than as integrating man with man and man with all life in some creative thrust. (One wonders about the amount of biology even in Schopenhauer's avowedly "metaphysical" argument for the noumenal unity of man, the problem of seeing personality as "maya" to be penetrated by the initiate.) All critics see "creative evolution" in *The Dynasts*, with its conception of blind Will gradually becoming conscious; but no one other than Gose has, to my knowledge, seen the importance of this emphasis in Hardy's *entire* reaction to Darwin, early and late.

Gose sees Tess as the failure of "psychic evolution" toward some ultimate form of altruism for all living creatures, a failure confirmed by her murder of Alec. I need not summarize his article here, though it is the only place in Hardy criticism where the impact of Darwin and the comparative and evolutionary anthropologists (particularly Tylor in *Primitive Culture*, 1871, and Frazer in his early *Totemism*, 1887) is vividly imagined. To put the matter with what little simplicity it allows, Hardy was much given to thinking about evolution in its creative aspect and to speculating in fictive ways about the modification of natural evolutionary laws by man's self-conscious grasp of them and by ethical qualities emerging as "variations." Most of the Spencerian social analysis according to evolutionary principles was foreign to Hardy, who apparently took to heart Darwin's admonition that "In social animals it [natural selection] will adapt the structure of each individual for the benefit of the community."[9] Still, Hardy's emphasis on the kinship of all creatures in an evolutionary way rather than on the ruthless struggle for existence (the Schopenhauerian Will surely resembles some aspects of this struggle) did not simply produce in him a straightforward desire to imagine charcters in whom this "psychic evolution" toward some ultimate altruism could take place. If Tess's killing the wounded birds is evidence of some such capacity in her, it also suggests some of the dark implications of our aboriginal kinship with all life. The self-reflective, self-conscious mind of man is apparently necessary to sense this evolutionary kinship—yet it may be precisely this capacity that definitively separates us from other forms of life.

I depart from Elliot Gose when he uses his splendid sense of Hardy's involvement with the comparative and evolutionary anthropologists to call Tess a failed psychic evolution. It is no exaggeration to say that Hardy brooded fictively on the dramatic essence of the "struggle for existence" and—Spencer's phrase before it was Darwin's—the "survival of the fittest." Darwin seems to have been as much aware of and concerned about the metaphoric nature of that word "struggle" as Stanley Edgar Hyman was in his comments on *The Origin of Species*.[10] The usually quiet drift toward existence or death on the "tangled bank" occasionally becomes, in Hardy, literally a tragic struggle of some kind of intrinsically natural man or woman to survive in a world where society has confusingly changed the less ambiguous rules of survival in nature. Thus in Tess we see her real affinities with basic natural processes, her limited but important participation in an ancient form of folk culture, her introduction to the byways and perversions of "modern" society, especially as Alec manifests them (and as they are symbolically rendered in connection with Alec and the modern threshing machine in that famous scene), and finally her betrayal by an imagined denial of modern society in Angel's Hellenic nature worship. Significantly, it is really only Angel's denial of any truly Darwinian knowledge of Nature that brings Tess down. Hardy imaginatively and systematically scrutinizes the idea of survival and indeed the whole question of who is fittest among

human beings by subjecting Tess to, as it were, degrees of societal complication and changes in the quality and texture of societal complication.
Angel's antisocietal idealism, it seems to me, is finally revealed as the
most potent corruption of society.

Angel's insistence on Tess's "newness" thus becomes wrong and destructive for her precisely because Tess is designed by Hardy to be definitively well suited for survival—*provided* that she is not confronted with an
actual nemesis. Of course this novel is conceived so that she is not granted
that favor. The novel is in a sense a controlled experiment whose outcome
is by no means a foregone conclusion for Hardy. Her survival qualities are
for me her most essential characteristics. Tough, resilient, healthy, loyal
and persevering, bright enough and yet not too bright, capable of guilt and
remorse yet not given to them (so that she can survive in more than a brut-
ish way, in a distinctly human way but not at all in a Christian fashion), a
lover with great staying power but no fool and not at all sentimental, Tess
is some kind of peculiarly *human* survival ideal—provided we do not finally undercut her entire nature with Christian ideals and with Angel's exact perversion of her identification as a natural, a truly natural creature.
Some critics have seen Tess as eminently unsuited for survival if we compare her with a Spencerian evolutionary ideal. But "adaptation" as Darwin
ambiguously used the word is a complex set of harmonics between environment and creature and not at all the ruthless triumph of strength and
cunning, or even of fortitude (understood in a vaguely ethical sense), as
Joseph Conrad and Stephen Crane developed the idea in "Falk" and "The
Open Boat."[11]

Tess now seems to me at least partly Hardy's answer to the following
question. Suppose man had not passed beyond heliolatry or beyond the ill-
defined folk culture that is not so far removed from its pagan origins in
Stonehenge and that survives in a debased form all around Tess. Suppose
she had not been victimized by a Christian *talent* for ideals that generate
guilt and remorse and, perhaps even worse, forgiveness as their psychological focus. And suppose, finally, that we are not talking about "survival" totally in some mindless, brutal way (as the d'Urbervilles survived quite a
long time by human measure), but as a quality which both depends on and
furthers the peculiar essence of whatever species is surviving, and in man
would at least mean survival with some sensitivity, self-consciousness, and
awareness of our evolutionary kinship with all life. Who then would be the

ideal of survival, understood now in its subtlest Darwinian sense of a symbiosis with the environment that causes the species's *unique qualities* not only to flourish but to flower to the point, as Darwin sometimes said, of downright "happiness"? (At rare moments Darwin liked to see this as the outcome of the "struggle.")[12]

It is in this sense that Tess is a victim of modern society and of Angel's denial of her true, truly Darwinian affinities with Nature. The geological and paleontological modes that Hardy uses to suggest her ancientness and the ideal quality of her consciousness are the antidote to Angel's claim of her newness, the antidote, however, that is never allowed to work. She really does come home, then, to Stonehenge a *pagan*, but the term is understood best by Hardy's suggestion in this novel that Tess is the *ideal* pagan, evolved beyond the paganism of her "noble" and nominally Christian ancestors and their Spencerian type of survival.

Before she meets Alec, she is capable of that peculiarly Darwinian "happiness" of a species so attuned to its total environment (Nature and limited forms of rustic society, in the case of Tess) that its essence flourishes and even rejoices, whatever that essence may be. One thinks of the animal poems of Ted Hughes. Yet Hardy, going I think beyond Hughes, has at least begun to imagine a fulfillment for man analogous to that possible for other species. Humans in Hughes's poems are always seen in contrast to the total self-possession of the animal (really an equality of possession: the self of the environment and the environment of the self), of the "pike" in that marvelous poem. The human in his very self-consciousness is unnatural, alienated (to repeat the modern clichés) from self itself. Had Tess not been born into a world where the steam-thresher and Alec and Angel dominate, the ideal pagan might at least have gone home to Stonehenge as a genuine sacrifice to the sun, and thus no victim at all.

As Stanley Edgar Hyman has argued, the spiritual impetus of *The Origin of Species* is toward teleology, toward the perfection of species. Even death is rationalized as "a trait evolved by natural selection, permitting a speedier improvement of the higher organisms, and thus an advantage in competition and a good for life."[13] But what is this "perfection" for man? Certainly to Hardy's sensibility it meant what Hyman calls Darwin's ultimate mystery,

> a kind of totemic brotherhood, a consubstantiality with all organic beings, resembling St. Paul's "every one members of one another."

In his contribution to *Darwin and Modern Science*, Frazer notes that when Europeans first landed on one of the Alaskan islands, the natives took them for cuttlefish on account of the buttons on their clothes. In a deeper sense, Darwin identifies Europeans as totemic brothers to cuttlefish, and reminds that what he calls in an early notebook "animals, our fellow brethren," are as precious as we in the eyes of our common mother.[14]

Manifest in a hundred small and large ways, this sense of evolutionary oneness with life is Tess's great virtue, though neither she nor Hardy has ever thought of Nature as "mother." But more significantly, it would also have been her main survival value (as the ecologically minded say it may be ours) and the truly Darwinian happiness open to her save for its defeat by the strategically designed bane of Angel's "naturalism." It is almost as though Hardy were suggesting (and this I find one of the most compelling thoughts in all his work) that this awareness of the evolutionary complicity of all life and all time and, perhaps (stripping Tylor and Frazer of their Victorian chauvinism), all culture is precisely the essence toward which evolution has driven man. Our perfect adaptation depends on this awareness. It is at once man's definitive self-consciousness (which so often in Conrad and Hardy seems antithetical to Nature and aghast at Nature's lack of moral purpose) and his identification with Nature. It is perhaps the only variety of mental awareness that does not isolate man from Nature. In its flowering (as it might easily have flowered in Tess), it is fundamentally both natural and moral, ideal and material, a conjunction which usually eluded both Hardy and Conrad and which Hardy had worried endlessly in *The Woodlanders*. To have possessed it fully would have been analogous to another creature so perfectly adapted to its environment that its biological "essence" was perfectly expressed in everything it did. In a sense, man would have come home.

Such, and no less, was the vision of Darwin and the evolutionary, comparative anthropologists pushed to its mystical extremity. I am greatly tempted to believe that in *Tess of the d'Urbervilles* Hardy had contemplated its frustration partly to see if he could imagine it at all. It will thus be seen that Angel's great sin has become really central for Hardy. In refusing to accept Tess's experience, in continuing to see her imagined newness irretrievably stained by the seduction, he is denying the definitive capacity of Nature to be infinitely old and experienced and yet forever new and virginal—not only in the sense of the "perennial philosophy" and the great cycle of seasons, but in the sense that the Darwinian perfection of the human species demands our sympathy for all truly natural behavior. One of the most courageous things Hardy had done in writing *Tess* was to refuse to make this seduction another drugged Clarissa, though he apparently flirted with this idea in the manuscript. Even a Victorian audience cannot deny Tess her right to be first of all a country girl.

In Tess the achievement of this Darwinian perfection—had Hardy continued to imagine it—would presumably have meant not only the fulfillment of her natural sympathy for all creatures (a fact which has led some critics to call her unsuited for survival, as I have said) but more importantly a sort of comprehensive evolutionary awareness—a way of including her natural qualities, her folk roots, and the d'Urberville inheritance in an intuitive sense of a larger identity "in Nature's teeming family" (232). One of the great mistakes possible in reading this novel is to take Tess's famous compassion for animals as just another mildly interesting aspect of her character. For one thing, that compassion must somehow be integrated with the fierceness that is equally her characteristic (if she sympathizes with the wounded birds, she does equally break their necks). Presumably Tess might have been something that would have risen not "above" love for Angel but certainly above his application of the notorious double standard and—crucially—well above his attempt to make this ancient creature new in his own naive sense. Her sympathy for animals is a sign of the great and extremely subtle Darwinian bias with which Hardy created her. It must be explained in her character according to Hardy's whole understanding of the evolutionary state of mind and of what Darwin meant by the perfection of species and the possible perfection of man.

Thus Hardy's apparently digressive essay when Tess finds herself among the wounded birds is no digression at all:

> She had occasionally caught glimpses of these men in girlhood, looking over hedges, or peering through bushes, and pointing their guns, strangely accoutred, a bloodthirsty light in their eyes. She had been told that, rough and brutal as they seemed just then, they were not like this all the year round, but were, in fact, quite civil persons save during certain weeks of autumn and winter, when, like the inhabitants of the Malay Peninsula, they ran amuck, and

made it their purpose to destroy life—in this case harmless feath-
ered creatures, brought into being by artificial means solely to grat-
ify these propensities—at once so unmannerly and so unchivalrous
toward their weaker fellows in Nature's teeming family. (232)

Some readers find Hardy's rhetoric here offensive, coming as it does during
a crucial moment in the dramatic rather than authorial exposition of Tess.
And the passage has usually been dismissed as one of Hardy's philosophic
meanderings, hardly integrated with the dramatic action at hand, though
the actual gesture of breaking the birds' necks is widely admired by critics.
   It must be said, however, that whether he has succeeded or not, Hardy
intended these feelings about the hunters to be a very important part of
Tess's character. We can hardly read the phrase "Nature's teeming family"
without seeing in it Hardy's Darwinian emphasis on the incredible relatedness of all creatures. The hunters seem to revert to an earlier, more primitive identity for which they nonetheless *artificially* raise their quarry. The
incongruity is genuinely shocking to Hardy. The whole passage is evolutionary not in a Spencerian way but as Hardy understood Darwin—and as
he would have had Tess feel the evolutionary consciousness. And, even
more important, that way of feeling establishes a correspondence with processes that go beyond living creatures to the rocks and the cosmos.

HARDY SAYS in the "Apology" to *Late Lyrics and Earlier* in 1922:

> Whether the human and kindred animal races survive till the ex-
> haustion or destruction of the globe . . . pain to all upon it, tongued
> or dumb, shall be kept down to a minimum by loving-kindness, op-
> erating through a scientific knowledge.[15]

Hardy's "evolutionary meliorism" (his own phrase in the "Apology") is familiar enough to students of *The Dynasts:* his occasional hope that the
consciousness of man will eventually redeem an Unconscious that has
dreamed or obscurely willed this world. But as this quotation indicates,
whether or not man's conscious morality can alter the Unconscious, Hardy
looks to a sympathy, a "loving-kindness" that seems to many readers of

The Dynasts to be of the most ordinary, humanistic variety. That the career of so distinguished a novelist should descend to this homily is disappointing to many. Yet if we are sensitive to the motives behind such phrases as "and kindred animal races," "tongued and dumb," "operating through a scientific knowledge," it will be clear that Hardy in this comment made thirty years after the publication of *Tess* is once more speaking of the peculiar turn of consciousness he gave us in *Tess*, a consciousness that he had labored at over the years in his attention to the traditional pastoral and its main virtue of otium. Here and in *Tess* that ancient contentment and rapprochement has developed into the extraordinary evolutionary sympathy for all life that makes Tess so magnificently self-possessed and pagan and Angel so definitely wrong in his conception of nature and newness.

Above all, we must see that Hardy's "loving-kindness" is not the refuge of an exhausted old man nor the cliché lurking in an otherwise experimental *Dynasts*. It is, on the contrary, the result of a remarkable ontological sensitivity working over a period of at least twenty years from *Under the Greenwood Tree* to *Tess of the d'Urbervilles*. It represents to Hardy the possible reconciliation of science and feeling, and of morality and science, for Darwin too had sensed the ultimate and perhaps unique identity of man lying in his profound discovery that he was not unique. No one other than Hyman has suggested just how happy this made Darwin or, I might add, how close to the ancient otium it brought him. As that pastoral virtue had always been opposed to ambition and vanity, so too in Darwin and Hardy it found once again its ancient antagonist. The overweening vanity of man's faith in his unique creation and, indeed, as Lovejoy suggests, in the whole "chain of being" was shattered. In its place—created with great difficulty by both men—a new humility fit to rival the Christian virtue arose when man took his proper place in "nature's teeming family." The strongest quality in Tess is her unprecedented self-possession. Baptizing her own child, breaking the birds' necks, murdering Alec, savoring contentedly her remaining time with Angel, she is at one with herself as only an acolyte of the primal otium could be, humble in an identity infinitely greater than any modern conception of ego, and yet assertive, on occasion, with the most extraordinary calm.

Even early in his career, Hardy had impressive imaginative glimpses of this primal otium. In *A Pair of Blue Eyes*, only his second novel, the character one critic calls "a brooding, restive intellectual"[16] falls and hangs over a cliff, apparently about to plunge to his death. Although the sum of Knight's trying experience suggests that Nature is positively hostile to man, rather than merely indifferent ("a feline fun in her tricks, begotten by a foretaste of her pleasure in swallowing the victim"), the heart of the description implies something far more important to our appreciation of Hardy's development from 1873 and *A Pair of Blue Eyes* to 1890 and *Tess of the d'Urbervilles*. Perry Meisel believes the passage offers "a black vision of the universe and of man's place in the cosmos, seen with the certainty offered only by death, free from any attempt to order the blinding chaos of human experience."[17] The text itself, however, suggests a remarkably early presaging of the evolutionary kinship that so distinguishes *Tess*.

As Knight hangs near death, the instinctive sequence of his thoughts implies a very curious and compelling, though as yet undeveloped, ordering of what is only apparently the chaos of man's experience. It is true that both Hardy and Knight see the fossil that soon catches his attention as Nature somehow "baiting" man, toying with him. But there is another more complex aspect of Nature revealed in Knight's elaborate reaction:

> By one of those familiar conjunctions of things wherewith the inanimate world baits the mind of man when he pauses in moments of suspense, opposite Knight's eyes was an imbedded fossil, standing forth in low relief from the rock. It was a creature with eyes. The eyes, dead and turned to stone, were even now regarding him. It was the single instance within reach of his vision of anything that had ever been alive and had had a body to save, as he himself had now.
>
> The creature represented but a low type of animal existence, for never in their vernal years had the plains indicated by those numberless salty layers been traversed by an intelligence worthy of the name. Zoophytes, mollusks, shellfish were the highest developments of those ancient dates. The immense lapses of time each formation represented had known nothing of the dignity of man. They were grand times, but they were mean times too, and mean were their relics. He was to be with the small in his death.
>
> Knight was a fair geologist: and such is the supremacy of habit over occasion, as a pioneer of the thoughts of men, that at this dreadful juncture his mind found time to take in, by a momentary

sweep, the varied scenes that had had their day between this creature's epoch and his own. There is no place like a cleft landscape
for bringing home such imaginings as these.

The time closed up like a fan before him. He saw himself at one
extremity of the years, face to face with the beginning and all the
intermediate centuries simultaneously. Fierce men, clothed in the
hides of beasts, and carrying, for defense and attack, huge clubs and
pointed spears, rose from the rock like the phantoms before the
doomed Macbeth. They lived in hollows, woods, and mud huts—
perhaps in caves of the neighboring rocks. Behind them stood an
earlier band. No man was there. Huge elephantine forms, the mas-
todon, the hippopotamus, the tapir, antelopes of monstrous size,
the megatherium, and the myledon—all, for the moment, in juxtaposition. Further back, and overlapped by these, were perched
huge-billed birds and swinish creatures as large as horses. Still
more shadowy were the sinister crocodilian outlines—alligators
and other uncouth shapes, culminating in the colossal lizard, the
iguanodon. Folded behind these were dragon forms and clouds of
flying reptiles: still underneath were fishy beings of lower development; and so on, till the lifetime scenes of the fossil confronting
him were a present and modern condition of things. These images
passed before Knight's inner eye in less than half a minute, and he
was again considering the actual present. (241–42)

All this evolutionary panorama is far from suggesting the *chaos* of
man's existence. The eyes of the trilobite imply that this elementary creature and the philosopher and critic Knight share the not insubstantial fact
that it too once had a body to save. The sentence "He was to be with the
small in his death," aside from being one of the most beautiful in Hardy, is
tremendously suggestive. The idea of death reduces (or elevates) one to a
fundamental awareness not of the differences between these lower forms
and man but, as the remarkable evolutionary bias of the passage indicates,
of the continuity. It is in the nature of Knight's intellectual pride, and of his
dominant role in the growing relationship with Elfride, to emphasize that
these lower forms had no "intelligence worthy of the name" and that these
eons had "known nothing of the dignity of man." Knight, as his name would
suggest, is an extremely proud man, jealous of man's most delicate capacity

for reflective thought and feeling. Even Knight, however, feels that these "mean times" with their mean relics were also, in another sense, "grand times." The whole magnificent scene on the cliff has been reversed, turned upside down by Hardy. The wind runs up the cliff, rises in an arch over the top, and finally touches the cliff behind anyone standing on the brink. It is, as Knight points out, an upside-down Niagara. It rains *up* on him:

> The world was to some extent turned upside down for him. Rain ascended from below. Beneath his feet was aerial space and the unknown; above him was the firm, familiar ground, and upon it all that he loved best. (244–45)

By analogy, other things are reversed: his pride in human uniqueness is punctured by the impending death, where he would be "with the small." Like the "lower" forms of life, he too has a body to save and a distinct place in the drama. A kind of evolutionary bathos controls the whole scene, and we are led to believe that as his consciousness reaches a moment when the "lifetime scenes of the fossil confronting him were a present and modern condition of things," Knight and Hardy have reached a level of insight into the meaning of man's and life's past that could not in Hardy's work be brought to even a frustrated conclusion for twenty years. Clearly there is almost nowhere in this plot for Knight's perception to go. It is too potent an insight for *A Pair of Blue Eyes*, though Knight is the outsider and modern man whom Hardy habitually opposes to the representative of "traditional order" (as Meisel calls him). Knight's heirs are Troy and Fitzpiers and Angel Clare and even Sue. He has a long way to go.

Simply in terms of plot, Knight's intellectual and emotional dominion over Elfride are all salvaged, and his life saved, by this girl who "seemed as small as an infant" (249) (small partly because she has managed to strip off nearly all her clothes and tie them into a rope). The very small rescues the proud philosopher in the most endearing yet curiously bathetic way. Throughout all this—the fossil, the evolutionary *tour de force*, the reverse Niagara, the rescue by intimate items of apparel knotted together—Knight's disdain for the eons when there was no man is curiously undercut by such infinitely resonant remarks as "Time closed up like a fan before him."

I have already shown how, throughout Hardy, time is meant to both open and close like a fan. Knight, like other proud knight-like characters entering the pastoral world for hundreds of years before him, is given at least a glimpse of another virtue that requires humility, self-possession beyond ego, and a rapprochement with a Nature here extended and deepened into evolutionary vistas.

Meisel argues that Knight's perception of the "chaos" and meaninglessness of existence and his attainment of a kind of antisocial omniscience characteristic of the author himself constitute a "disturbing impulse" for Hardy.[18] In dismissing Knight's perception on the cliff without any significant development, Hardy, says Meisel, is in effect repressing his desire to stand with the individual against the community, to favor the truth of individual perceptiveness, lack of illusions, and even cynicism against the settled expectations of the traditional order (exemplified quite well by Gabriel Oak in the next novel Hardy would write). Meisel reminds us that this quality is just what D. H. Lawrence dislikes in Hardy, that, as Lawrence says, Hardy

> must stand with the average against the exception, he must, in his ultimate judgment, represent the interests of humanity, or the community as a whole, and rule out the individual interest.
>
> To do this, however, he must go against himself. His private sympathy is always with the individual against the community: as in the case with the artist.[19]

As impressive as Meisel's attention to this remarkable passage in *A Pair of Blue Eyes* may be, Knight's perception on the cliff is not an ultimately antisocial glimpse of "the horror." Its incredible emphasis on relatedness and continuity indicates that if Hardy represents the interests of the community against the individual, it is because even at this early date he has a remarkably expanded and subtle sense of what "community" may ultimately mean under the pressure of evolutionary and anthropological ways of thinking. More important, he has begun to see that individuality must be based upon more than ego, more even than the sort of artistic, omniscient, prophetic ego that Lawrence implies. In this emphasis, he is more than sympathetic with the ancient pastoral of the self and with pastoral phenomenological humility in general. What he foresees, however, is not a program of bringing society into alignment with man's natural identity. Even in *Jude the Obscure* and *Tess of the d'Urbervilles*, the reform of society is secondary to the creation of new forms of consciousness that allow man at least glimpses of a larger society. Who but Hardy would, in the 1870s, have put that long, visionary, evolutionary meditation in the middle of a mediocre love story—and have made it at least partly work? And who but Hardy could have intimated that such an insight would have anything to do with love?

In *Tess*, however, we have one of the most remarkable attempts since the early Romantics to revolutionize consciousness itself, to suggest that beneath loving and reforming and even our view of dying lies the changing mode of consciousness. Calling Tess's peculiar turn of consciousness "evolutionary" may seem to slight the fact that Hardy was an artist and that what we are talking about is symbolic form and not scientific method. I think, however, that Tess's quality of consciousness is shared by Hardy's own imaginative processes, so that we all know, in the very metaphoric texture of the language and in the least feature of the symbolic form, that in her capture among the megaliths Tess would welcome the idea that she too was "to be with the small."

As it was even in *A Pair of Blue Eyes*, such a perception is anything but out of place in a love story. For Hardy, as for Darwin, the trilobite may evoke a humility in man that gives dignity to the fossil not as a small step on the way to human consciousness but as a Hardian substitute for the Christian fallen sparrow. It is in this vein, in this *projet*—to use Sartre's term—that Hardy's consciousness moves most subtly and imperceptibly into questions of love, and it is in this phenomenological sensitivity that Tess's love finds its autochthonous toughness and range. Harold Tolliver has speculated that "successful pastoral ordinarily discovers an elementary link 'of man with all beings as beings, vague as to its special content, but far-embracing and generalizing.'"[20] Surely Knight and the fossil, Hardy and the fossil, are as close to a reunion of "beings as beings" as we are likely to get anywhere in the century, and Tess even in her defeat is not far behind in the intensity of her related accomplishment. Tolliver's description may indeed be our most effective way of grasping what is so special about *Tess* as a novel: the ease with which we move from geological descriptions to human personality, from genealogy to paleontology, from fiction to the very metaphoric texture of science. In the true pastoral spirit we have entered a realm where the processes of the natural world, usually described by science or by Oaks and Winterbornes in their fashion, are not easily distinguished from those of the personal and social world, usually described by poets and novelists. We are dealing, as Tolliver says, with an "elemental being" so easily dissipated by antipastoral forms that we doubt it ever really existed.

And we are in a position to understand in more ordinary terms the apparent mysticism of such passages as this from the Fore Scene to *The Dynasts*:

> A new and penetrating light descends on the spectacle, embuing men and things with a seeming transparency, and exhibiting as one organism the anatomy of life and movement in all humanity and vitalized matter.[21]

Men and things, humanity and "vitalized" matter are seen to interpenetrate one another in a manner that arises from the long exploration of the pastoral in Hardy's work. The processes of things and the processes of the lives of men, of consciousness itself, coalesce in a spirit that is less mystical than it is the fruit of the best phenomenological method of the age. Tylor and Darwin are no less Prospero in all this than are Schopenhauer, Von Hartmann, and the transforming imagination of Hardy himself. Above all, however, we must avoid seeing the spirit of *The Dynasts* quoted above as a kind of philosophical *deus ex machina* borrowed by Hardy rather late in his life and largely irrelevant to his great accomplishment in the fiction. It represents, on the contrary, a hard-won state of mind, evolved imaginatively through many of his best novels. In the way this passage, and indeed most of *The Dynasts*, joins "men and things" we have a profound linking of the ancient pastoral with the most advanced evolutionism and phenomenology. Hardy himself, however, would surely not have described things so formally and would no doubt be content to remember that if man too was a "survival," he had at least survived long enough to hear the prophecy of his return. In a culture where both idealists and empiricists had managed to isolate consciousness, Hardy and Lawrence did as much as Husserl and Heidegger to imagine a world reaching out to consciousness as much as consciousness sought the world.

Five
Jude the Obscure

In the pastoral context I have suggested, Tess eludes tragedy. Indeed, most readers do not think of her as a tragic heroine, nor does Hardy himself provide the allusions that surround such likely candidates as Clym or Henchard. It remains to be shown that Jude too ought to be understood in this same great pastoral vein, as a defeated pastoral hero whose developing goal lies clearly in the direction of the green world. But by this time in his career Hardy had come to see the green world not as a time or place or even as a way of life, but as a distinct mode of consciousness engaged in a mortal struggle with the demands of modernism. If Matthew Arnold's pat phrase "imaginative reason" seemed inadequate to Hardy as a description of what modernism already was, it nonetheless spoke to the right anxiety: that modernism had somehow allowed the whole human spirit to become fragmented, Sue Bridehead herself to become—as I shall show—the false shepherd. The "reason" which told Hardy he lived in an indifferent universe and was, like Jude, at best a victim could not be allowed to exist apart from the "imagination" which led to obscure alternatives but nonetheless "to fresh woods, and pastures new." Reason was the usurper, as William Blake had warned, who claimed in cold logic that its ontology superseded all others.

As *Jude the Obscure* opens, the schoolmaster—with all his fragile links to the classical past through Latin and Greek literature—is leaving a village where the archaeological and traditional past is largely obliterated. The well shaft that Jude stares down "was probably the only relic of the local history that remained absolutely unchanged" (16).[1] If in one sense Oxford's failure to embrace Jude is a flaw of society, then *Jude the Obscure* is a novel of intense social criticism of both that lapse and of the marriage laws and mores. But in another sense, *Jude the Obscure* is a novel about the failure of "learning" to provide those harmonic sympathies which distinguish Tess as a heroine and so often in Hardy are associated with these "relics."

The original church, "hump-backed" and a virtual palimpsest of local tradition, has been demolished in favor of a modern Gothic church (a style "unfamiliar to English eyes" and eccentric to the site and the local architectural styles), designed by "a certain obliterator of historic records who had run down from London and back in a day" (16). Hardy now calls the old church "the ancient temple to the Christian divinities" in order to emphasize the continuity between pagan temples and Christian churches: as in his poem "Aquae Sulis," various gods are needed from time to time; there is no "progress" in man's religion. The graves are now marked by cheap cast-iron crosses "warranted to last five years" (16).

Of course Hardy is bitter at all this loss, but we must also notice that he is presenting us with a hero similarly deprived; far more than ancient graves and buildings is at stake for both Hardy and Jude. A peculiar deracination has now become possible for a sensitive pastoral character such as Jude, who resembles Tess but cannot match her fierce naturalness. Deprived of harmonic sympathies with the past, Jude is attracted to books as a yet uncompromised source of a related quality. Although his great-aunt simply claims that his love of books "runs in our family, rather" (18), Jude apparently seeks in books something similar to what Tess inarticulately senses all around her. Jude is presented in these early pages as a boy who instinctively finds a freshly plowed field an "ugly" place, "Taking away its gradations, and depriving it of all history beyond that of a few recent months" (18–19). Nonetheless, even this field is actually freighted with some of the ancient continuities we have come to expect in Hardy's places; as he explains at some length, he finds echoes of songs from ancient harvest days and of love carelessly given or given in many forms by countless generations.

For Hardy the whole rural scene is increasingly like the demolished church and plowed field. Unlike any of Hardy's earlier rustic heroes, Jude has no ready access to the past or to the earth. Even Clym, though he is a long way from the fundamental Oak or Winterborne, can find some of these elemental sympathies in the outcast heath. Jude feels some kinship with the birds he has been hired to frighten away: "A magic thread of fellow-feeling united his own life with theirs," and not only because his life is "as puny and sorry" as theirs (20). Phillotson's last words to the boy yoked learning with kindness to animals in a way that needs to be explained on the basis of a special Darwinism in Hardy: "Be a good boy, remember; and be kind to animals and birds, and read all you can" (15). One is tempted to see this remark as only another compulsive instance of Hardy's well-known feelings about animals, yet we remember how thoroughly such comments were integrated in *Tess of the d'Urbervilles* and how potent a clue they are to the sympathies that charge that novel. So they are here.

True to his own inclination and to Phillotson's advice ("Mr. Phillotson said I was to be kind to 'em——O, O, O!"), Jude allows the birds to eat and is soundly punished by the farmer who owns the field and who has contributed handsomely to building the new church. The "brand-new church tower" echoes to the beating that Jude endures, and the whole scene persuades Jude painfully that he lives in a seriously flawed universe "by which what was good for God's birds was bad for God's gardener" (21). In the ideal pastoral state, the interest of God's birds and God's gardener is identical; comic though it may partly be, Jude's perception is of a crucially anti-pastoral condition that is associated in these early pages and throughout the novel with the demolished record of an organic past and with the deracination of sensitive country folk who have lost those ancient sympathies. At least the natives of Egdon Heath still have their bonfires and mumming; even if the symbolic meaning has been lost to any articulate awareness, it survives intuitively. The countryside of *Jude the Obscure*, however, has gone well along toward this lobotomy, toward this autocracy of the present.

The rather famous conclusion of chapter 2 has always been mined for its disillusioned Darwinism and its reconstruction of Hardy's boyhood experience of pulling the straw hat over his face and musing that, given the flawed scheme of things, he simply did not want to grow up. We are given in detail Jude's sympathy toward suffering worms, young birds, and cut trees and move on toward Hardy's conclusion that anyone so sensitive could be expected to suffer a great deal. The dark litany of the chapter peaks with Hardy's and Jude's Jobian indictment of creation: "Nature's logic was too horrid for him to care for. That mercy toward one set of creatures was cruelty toward another sickened his sense of harmony" (23).

Although critics have always seen Hardy's outrage at the "survival of the fittest" lurking in these remarks, what ought to be emphasized is the sense that having failed to discover these crucial harmonies either in the demolished ancient survivals of the countryside or in a Spencerian scheme of nature, Hardy and Jude immediately appear to relocate them in the symbol of Christminster. The "harmony," the ultimate sympathy for all life as "members of one body" that comes almost as an epiphany in *Tess*, is clearly impossible for Jude or for Hardy in this novel. Sensitive to the suffering of all life much in the way that Tess is, Jude does not have that natural quality of the "friendly leopard" that puts Tess in genuinely true correspondence and consonance with these forces and seems always to leave Jude on the outside looking in. Although Jude kills the trapped rabbit almost as neatly as Tess does the wounded birds, he has none of her characteristic "fierceness." All this we sense almost immediately in *Jude the Obscure*. Tess seduced by Alec and Jude seduced by Arabella produce markedly different results: Tess's infinitely renewable innocence is rather quickly and naturally reestablished as she gravitates toward the valley of the great dairies; Jude will characteristically regard his taste for Arabella as something gross and beyond the pale of his true character. Trying not to step on any of the "coupled" earthworms, he is somehow abstractly beyond absorbing the reason for their coupling. Yet unquestionably some sense of "correspondence" is far from dead either in Jude himself or in Hardy's expectations of what he may be able to express in Jude's life.

One of the crucial problems of this novel, then, is whether Jude fails because of society's and Oxford's shortcoming (whether we have a true "reform" novel), or whether the failure does not lie in Jude's faith in learning and Sue Bridehead. We are accustomed to seeing in the luminous symbol of Christminster (looking in the distance like "the heavenly Jerusalem") a mixture of Jude's desire for learning with a youthful, romantic enthusiasm to escape home and enter a larger social world. What we have not yet seen is the extent to which this holy city rises on Jude's horizon after the ancient church has been demolished and replaced, the field of the past plowed for the last time, and the Icknield Street and original Roman road finally abandoned even by flocks and herds going to fairs; at this point Jude's larger sympathy for other forms of life survives only fitfully in the morass of his own suffering.

It may be useful to see Tess and Jude as different aspects of Hardy as he approaches this ultimate sense of "true correspondence": Tess in her unlearned way still able to draw upon a primal sympathy for the ancient folkways and for the natural world, Jude turning toward the world of learning and reason. We are justified in asking whether Hardy could have imagined finding in Oxford the vision of wholeness which Hardy always associated with the pastoral ideal (where what was good for God's birds was good for God's gardener). This much should at least become our benchmark: the ideal of Christminster, its very image, emerges from a complex first two chapters, where it takes shape in terms of the harmony Jude would like in Nature's scheme and against the background of the disappearing conduits to an organic sense of the past. It makes no more sense to dissociate Hardy's discussion of the demolished church, plowed field, sensitivity to the suffering of animals, and so on from his emerging vision of Christminster than it would to read *The Return of the Native* without any intuition that it is a variation of the ancient pastoral. When young Jude climbs the ladder for his view of the distant Jerusalem, we ought to remember that the ladder is grounded in a rather specific rural desolation and in a disillusioning Spencerianism. It must have seemed perfectly natural to Hardy that Phillotson should link kindness to animals with continued learning in his final advice to Jude. Both virtues involve the central perception that so permeates *Tess of the d'Urbervilles*. We ignore this rather peculiar association at the same risk that we ignore Tess's preoccupation with kindness to the creatures "in Nature's teeming family," as she calls it.

The only "survival" Jude attempts to use as a means of learning is Physician Vilbert, the itinerant quack who avoids all but the rustics: "He was, in fact, a survival" (31). Agreeing to gather orders for his various nostrums, Jude expects to be brought Vilbert's own Greek and Latin grammars. Of course Jude is disappointed; if Vilbert ever used such books he has no intention of fulfilling his bargain with Jude. In carefully pointing out that Vilbert is a survival, Hardy reminds us of the importance this concept has had throughout his work, and especially in *The Return of the Native*. Both Hardy and the reader intuitively know, however, that the "tree of knowledge" (31) which Jude now associates with Christminster is not the knowledge available through survivals, above all not through the debased survival represented by this quack. The reddleman too is a survival, as are the mumming and the bonfires; but all these still offer their runic meanings in some potent symbolic way. We may correctly see Vilbert as representative of the general decay of survivals in *Jude the Obscure*, a devolution that joins the opening discussion of the demolished church, the cheap iron crosses, and the plowed field in a portrait of decadence where only the least potent survivals remain.

Even as a debased survival, however, the quack raises a further problem: is there any sense in which even the most potent survival can lead one toward the sort of knowledge we associate with learning Greek and Latin grammar, "the tree of knowledge"? In closing to Jude the ancient conduits to a folk-pastoral vision, Hardy has known from the outset of this novel that Jude is to eat of the forbidden tree and fall into a knowledge revealingly unlike Tess's. Even the most promising survivals are as unscientific and procrustean as Vilbert's antique quackery. They have never offered anything like the knowledge obtainable in Christminster. So uncongenial is the Christminster Greek and Latin grammar to Jude's rustic intuitions, that he "assumed that the words of the required language were always to be found somewhere latent in the words of the given language by those who had the art to uncover them" (36). He is at least enough like Tess to have this essentially archaeological or paleontological view of current reality. One probes to uncover archaic forms shaping the present, as Joseph Conrad did at about the same time. Hardy says that Jude's mode here is an exaggeration of Grimm's Law, which is after all an evolutionary and genetic law, whose principle lay also at the basis of comparative mythology and evolutionary anthropology. The grammar he will learn in Christminster, or from the books he would have studied there, is merely descriptive and as unlike the comparative and genetic method as Linnaeus is unlike Darwin. Even Jude still has at least the seed of this Tess-like sensibility in him.

Despite the distraction of his passion for Arabella, Jude cannot, for example, stroll with her past "the circular British earth-bank" without "thinking of the great age of the trackway, and of the drovers who had frequented it, probably before the Romans knew the country" (64). This familiar sensibility apparently resembles for Hardy Jude's later sensitivity to the pig-sticking, which he performs himself, refusing to let the pig die slowly so as to bleed the meat properly. The blood of this "fellow-mortal" staining the snow evokes quite a profound emotional reaction in Jude: "The white snow, stained with the blood of his fellow mortal, wore an illogical look to him as a lover of justice, not to say a Christian" (76). These sympathies of present for past and man for other "mortals" (of life for all other *forms* of life) compose the truly natural cast of Jude's mind in contrast to the merely sensuous pragmatism of Arabella. Hardy's perspective throughout this elaborate contrast of Arabella's grossness with Jude's sensitivity is not, as many readers conclude, that Jude's refined feelings are somehow above and beyond the world of cruel natural survival (where pigs must die slowly because "poor folks must live" [75]), but that Jude is more significantly natural than Arabella. Although his life history amply suggests that he is by no means above the struggle for existence, he is open to those larger perspectives that constitute the perfection of his species. Hardy's use of the word "illogical" with regard to the death of the pig is quite remarkable and reveals an important aspect of Jude's character. That the term should be applied at all to a simple farmyard slaughtering of meat is at least surprising.

Hardy's tribute to Oxford is that it too can be a living organism where the past is always functional in the body of the living, as it obviously is in his and Jude's when describing the "ghosts" of the place; it can be analogous to Grimm's Law rather than to Linnaeus. At its worst it can be cruelly taxonomic in a variety of ways: in classifying young men as eternally workmen or tradesmen not allowed to hope for an Oxford education (as in the Master of Biblioll's advice to Jude), and perhaps even more significantly in using some crudely taxonomic sense of the past to deny the present and future. Thus Jude even in his reverent and complex attitude toward his own work on ancient buildings shows a disposition that modern thought sometimes rejects as thoroughly as it has medievalism:

> He did not at that time see that mediaevalism was as dead as a fernleaf in a lump of coal; that other developments were shaping in the world around him, in which Gothic architecture and its associations had no place. The deadly animosity of contemporary logic and vision towards so much of what he held in reverence was not yet revealed to him. (97)

Hardy's own taste for Gothic is amply shown in his *Architectural Notebook*, where he lovingly designs such items as a wrought-iron hinge and closing ring in the manner of the thirteenth century and records Gothic windows, fonts, and leaf sculpture for subsequent use in his own church restoration.[2] He had for a short time assisted the author of the popular *Analysis of Gothic Architecture* (1847), Raphael Brandon, and had set out as a young man to become expert in the Gothic church architecture he was to encounter in the restoration of Stinsford and St. Juliot. Most interesting for an appreciation of *Jude the Obscure*, however, is the fact that while Hardy was writing this novel he had undertaken the restoration of a small country church southeast of Dorchester called West Knighton. Two years earlier in 1889 he had seen, despite his own efforts, another local church "restored" nearly out of existence and had apparently decided that West Knighton was to be solely under his direction. It was—and Hardy managed to uncover and salvage numerous details of early Gothic architecture, including old arches with a remaining pillar, old frescoes, and inscriptions.

Hardy was later to write of his efforts: "As observed by Hutchins, it [West Knighton] contains nothing remarkable. This statement is not now correct. Recent examination and repairs have uncovered much interesting early architecture."

William Morris's manifesto for the Society for the Protection of Ancient Buildings (of which Hardy had long been an active member) insisted that old work should not be imitated in the process of restoration, that to do so would be dishonest and possibly deceiving to future generations. Paula Power has identical feelings in *A Laodicean*. Yet in restoring West Knighton, Hardy had precisely imitated three early English windows in an effort at preservation that was so impassioned it allowed him to violate one of the principles of his much respected Society. In this effort to uncover and preserve at all costs, one may see Hardy paralleling in architecture the value he would preserve in Jude, at the very moment he is writing *Jude*. In his earlier work on churches, Hardy had largely been at the mercy of other directing architects and builders and often felt guilty at what he had done. In West Knighton and in the whole imaginative conception of Jude as a character, this guilt is surely expiated. C. J. P. Beatty has argued nearly as much with great intelligence.

Yet the inestimable value of the independence and spontaneity which Hardy again and again said he found in old Gothic architecture is not relevant to *Jude the Obscure* in the way that Beatty suggests. When Hardy wrote that he considered "a social system based on individual spontaneity to promise better for happiness than a curbed and uniform one under which all temperaments are bound to shape themselves to a single pattern of living,"[3] he was reflecting both Sue and Jude. But when Beatty suggests that the Gothic spontaneity is built into both their characters he slights the fact that Sue's spontaneity and unfettered intelligence rejects the old Gothic, detests it, and will not look at it. She would cultivate her spontaneity with an ethereal "freedom" that Hardy, as Beatty points out, would not allow himself in the windows at West Knighton. The value in Jude, then, is that, like Hardy at West Knighton, he intuits that a sense of belonging to larger harmonies involving both the past and a capacious Nature may be more important than seizing every chance for individual spontaneity. In feeling this way, both Hardy and Jude may be closer to the true basis of the old Gothic than either knew: a cohesive society that nonetheless found a place for spontaneity.

Jude the Obscure

In the juxtaposition of Jude's barely surviving rural and pastoral sense of organicism with the "deadly animosity of contemporary logic and vision" to any such harmonic, Hardy was restating one of his own great personal problems, an anxiety that is woven throughout his life and art. The question behind much of *Jude the Obscure* is, I repeat, less whether Oxford will open its doors than whether Oxford itself has become another of these failed symbols of organicism and continuity. Jude occasionally sees the "true Illumination; that here in the stone yard was a centre of effort as worthy as that dignified by the name of scholarly study within the noblest of the colleges. But he lost it under the stress of his old idea [his aspiration toward learning] . . . ; but he would accept it [this job] as a provisional thing only. This was his form of the modern vice of unrest" (97). He is plagued by that ancient antagonist of the pastoral, the aspiring mind, unrest—"the modern vice" which has ancient roots.

If we ask in what sense the "effort" of the stonecutters was as worthy as that of the scholars within the walls of Oxford, clearly Hardy means to imply not only that all labor has dignity (perhaps in Carlyle's sense of "work"), or that there is so-called scholarship that is less than transcendent, but that such men as Jude, despite the degeneration of the countryside, may still have access to the sensitivity he has already demonstrated for the British earthwork earlier in the novel. When Jude stands in the ancient Oxford Crossway, the "other" Oxford still functions as the symbol of an ideal that has very possibly been lost in the university.

He only heard in part the policeman's further remarks, having fallen into thought on what struggling people like himself had stood at that Crossway, whom nobody ever thought of now. It had more history than the oldest college in the city. It was literally teeming, stratified, with the shades of human groups. (133)

And Hardy goes on to sweep this stratification from tragedy to farce, cursing to blessing, Napoleon to the arrival of Caesar in Britain. His use of the word "stratified" serves to connect this kind of sensibility with Tess's virtually geological sense of the dynamic stratification of her world.

He began to see that the town life was a book of humanity infinitely more palpitating, varied, and compendious than the gown life. These struggling men and women before him were the reality of Christminster, though they knew little of Christ or Minster. That was one of the humors of things. The floating population of students and teachers, who did know both in a way, were not Christminster in a local sense at all. (133)

Such comments are no rationalization for Jude's failure to penetrate the "gown" side of Christminster. Hardy, on the contrary, has mounted a comparison of the two Oxfords by way of exploring the modern university and the whole intellectual process for its failure to sustain those values he had first discovered in the rural world. We may legitimately wonder whether any scholarly and intellectual heritage could have done so, and whether Hardy's own life had not shown how poisonous the relentless logic of Mill or Darwin could at least potentially be to the chthonic sympathies of the pastoral. I have shown, however, that Hardy had occasionally come to see Darwin's lucid reason not as antithetical to these sympathies but as their fulfillment, and it is in this light that the modern Oxford, in Hardy's eyes at least, had disappointingly become the taxonomic totem of all England, classifying England's Judes out of existence and doing the same to the inestimable rustic heritage that engendered them.

There is always such tension in Hardy's life and work between folk roots and folk knowledge and the more-or-less official, scholarly learning that had early attracted him but that he never embraced. If this is a rhetorical novel about Oxford's failure to acknowledge plebeian Jude, it also implies, on a much larger scale, the inability of traditional scholastic learning to accommodate the ancient folk sensibility. We may speculate that Hardy's taste for the new comparative anthropology had something to do with its ability to effect precisely this cooperation of scholastic learning and ancient folkways. In any event, we will not find this richly "stratified" sense of life inside the walls but outside, in the "other" Christminster at the primeval Fourways. Mother of great thinkers of all persuasions and temperaments (as Jude's nocturnal review makes clear), Oxford is yet a place of contention and fragmentation, of a Christianity that will not go beneath and behind itself to—as it were—the pagan bubbling spring beneath the "baldachined altar." When Jude draws the workman's chalk from his pocket and writes on the college wall, "I have understanding as well as you," it is not really clear that the same kind of understanding is meant. As his then recent meditation at Fourways suggests, his understanding is quite different from even the most appealing Oxonians he has conjured up in his enthusiasm.

Robert Gittings in *Young Thomas Hardy* suggests that Hardy's reluctance to acknowledge his family's humble origins is more than common snobbery—that his motives went beyond class distinctions to suggest a fundamental tension in his mind between "reverence for learning" and "people of his own background, who, however full of simple wisdom, could literally not speak the language which Hardy had acquired. . . . In novels, he might extol the instinctive rightness of the peasant; in life, he always sought the company of the educated."[4] His brother Henry, on the contrary, retained a Dorset rusticity all his life, and without a trace of embarrassment. Jude's relations with Christminster, then, may suggest a seminal uneasiness within Hardy according to which his taste for learning represented some sort of irresistible loss (as with Clym Yeobright). That this learning, especially the evolutionism that permeated the thought and feeling of so many Victorian intellectuals, could lead *back* to these great aboriginal sympathies, that the circle could be closed elegantly, was the submerged hope that impels *Tess of the d'Urbervilles*.

The character of Sue Bridehead reflects this uneasiness through a "stratification" of Hardy's earlier work: she may be not only a version of Bathsheba but especially of the complex relationships between Eustacia, Clym, and the heath. Like the heath itself, Sue seems alternately the most modern thing (as the heath is the only landscape modern enough for Clym), attacking all "played out" forms and institutions, and, as she says, "not modern either. I am more ancient than mediaevalism, if you only knew" (151). Like Eustacia, she is an epicure of emotions, and both are passionate beyond sexual passion, although no one would accuse Eustacia of being "epicene," as Hardy does Sue. Still, there is a strong epicurean quality about Sue which places the same aesthetic distance between feelings and the savoring consciousness of feelings. Like Bathsheba, Sue resolutely refuses to define herself by love for a man or by marriage. She wants "modernism" no more than the medievalism—only the freedom to submit both to independent inquiry and judgment. When she and Jude spend a holiday together, her first wish is "Not ruins, Jude—I don't care for them" (153).

Without my exaggerating the contrast, this distaste for ruins runs counter to at least one aspect of Jude's sensitivity to the past. Sue's most comprehensive quality is the sense in which she becomes a wraith, dissociated from everything except an increasingly febrile need for a very abstract "freedom": freedom from sexual passion, from the past, from all "played out" forms, from marriage. She claims an affinity with pagan Greece and brings statues of the Greek gods into her room, and later in the novel will not visit the "Gothic ruins" of Wardour but is persuaded to do so when Jude tells her that Wardour is "quite otherwise. It is a classic building—Corinthian, I think" (153).

Yet it is far more accurate to say that she is an epicure of these more nearly neoclassical than pagan enthusiasms almost solely for their anti-church, iconoclastic value. When Sue is about to marry Phillotson the first time, she makes Jude walk her to the altar in what seems an almost sadistic act. "'I like to do things like this,' she said in the delicate voice of an epicure in emotions, which left no doubt that she spoke the truth." The epicureanism here is very reminiscent of Eustacia's, especially because Hardy sees it as the direct result of a kind of deracination: as Eustacia negates the mumming and all it suggests of submerged links with the past, the sophistication of her performance seems to substitute theatrical values for symbolic cultural ones. Eustacia's enthusiasm in life is for watching herself fill the role of the great romantic lover rather than for any direct accomplishment of that identity in the manner of Catherine or Heathcliff. Hardy implies that to be cut off from the continuities and sympathies that distinguish Clym, Tess, and the pastoral as a state of mind is, for certain personalities, to court an epicurean imitation of emotions rather than the direct feelings themselves. If Egdon Heath and Eustacia both contain a dialectic seminal to Hardy's work—a pair of opposites that intricately define one another—then as a character Sue is a strange combination of both the heath and Eustacia. Is she the most primitive thing imaginable or overcivilized to the point of decadence?

Hardy arranges a mock-pastoral interlude in order to explore the complexity of her role. Returning from their holiday they walk cross-country to intercept a train, "Jude cutting from a little covert a long walking-stick for Sue as tall as herself, with a great crook which made her look like a shepherdess" (154). Hardy is beginning to measure her peculiar sensitivity against the pastoral sensibilities of Jude, to see her if only momentarily as a potential inhabitant of the green world. They find themselves unable to reach the station and ask a real shepherd if they may rest in his cottage.

This man, perhaps the last of Hardy's vintage rustics, kindly suggests they stay overnight. He speaks nearly in dialect, and he and his toothless mother share their dinner of boiled bacon and greens with Jude and Sue. When dinner has been cleared away, Sue remarks: "I rather like this. . . . Outside all laws except gravitation and germination" (156). "'You only think you like it; you don't: you are quite a product of civilization,' said Jude, a recollection of her engagement reviving his soreness a little."

> "Indeed I am not, Jude, I like reading and all that, but I crave to get back to the life of my infancy and its freedom."
> "Do you remember it so well? You seem to have nothing unconventional at all about you."
> "O, haven't I! You don't know what's inside me."
> "What?"
> "The Ishmaelite."
> "An urban miss is what you are." (156)

It barely seems possible for Hardy to get through a novel without at least implying the term "Ishmaelite." The concept obviously had great significance for him, surely in connection with the idea of survivals, a term that as we have seen occurs with almost equal frequency. The passage above has usually been attributed to Jude's anger at Sue's engagement, at her unprecedented conventional behavior. It is often assumed that he scarcely means what he says. Yet I think we are intended to take his comment seriously despite his mood. Like Egdon, Sue has an intensely Ishmaelitish aspect; she is an outcast in so many ways, and in her usual unconventionality and iconoclasm also seems a kind of wild man. Nevertheless, as Jude properly detects, there is equally in her a quality that eventually makes her remarry Phillotson, come finally to his bed, and become the manic supporter of convention who brings Jude rapidly to his death.

She is not simply inconsistent. As the mock-pastoral vignette makes clear, Sue has no access to the pastoral state of mind, which she mistakes as being simply beyond all but natural physical law. As Jude says, she is an "urban miss" who mistakes the pastoral condition as "freedom from" rather than "sympathy for." If germination is truly one of the great pastoral laws, Sue gives birth grudgingly to children we know largely through their death at the hand of Little Father Time. Whatever fertility she may have is a dead end. She cherishes Little Father Time as though he were her own, for in her refusal of all but a Swinburnian rhetoric of the pagan past (a refusal of "ruins" and "played out" forms), she has perverted the pastoral sense of time and has in her own way, apart from the significance of Jude's and Arabella's bearing the child, created a definitive distortion of the time sense Hardy had been developing since *Under the Greenwood Tree.* She would "make it new" in the most radical sense, and though her criticisms of Oxford are often close to what Hardy himself might have said, "new wine in old bottles" (168), as she describes modern Oxford, is no disaster if one understands the need even for such makeshift continuity. Her intellect cuts and slashes (as when she very intelligently rearranges the New Testament), and she is the bane of Tess's intuitions. She seems incapable of becoming part of a tradition or of a culture stretching back in time. Her asexuality sets her apart from the very law of germination she finds so fundamental.

In having Jude cut her shepherdess's crook and conjure up one last time the pastoral hearth, Hardy has imagistically cast her out from the pastoral world. She suggests indeed the antipastoral. Jude, in his alternate need for and rejection of Arabella's earthy sexuality, at least roots himself in the sort of natural taste that Sue constantly etherealizes out of existence. When Sue finally reacts to Jude's accusation that she is an urban miss, a product not of the pastoral world but of sophisticated culture, she says:

> "You called me a creature of civilization, or something didn't you?" she said, breaking a silence. "It was very odd you should have done that."
> "Why?"
> "Well, because it is provokingly wrong. I am a sort of negation of it." (165)

Sue of course would like this comment to mean that she is the ultimate free spirit, destructive of all "played out" forms. She is Ishmaelite because society drives her out as a dangerous person who will not unquestioningly follow the dictates of custom and tradition. Hardy, however, in reminding us that she is definitively *not* the shepherdess, has passed beyond Sue's meaning to the apprehension that if both the author and reader value this Ishmaelite quality in her (and who could be more profoundly opposed to the tyranny of played-out sexual and marital laws and customs than

Hardy?), she is nonetheless a frightening soul who will be subversive of even the best sense of the term "civilization." In shaking off the bonds of society, she has apparently torn up the deeper irrational roots of culture and civilization and, in a sense she does not understand, has really become its "negation." Intellectually she knows where her culture, Western European culture, has been. But, as Jude increasingly sees, she has somehow lost the substance, the body and substantiality of life. In this she undercuts Tess as surely as she suggests the antipastoral. In loving and pursuing this noumenous energy, this ascetic flame, our rustic hero has encountered the only force that could draw him entirely out of the pastoral world. The maiming of Jude is accomplished about equally by Oxford's refusal, however useless its approval might have been, and Sue's strange deracination.

However ephemeral that green world may seem to us (and may have seemed to Hardy even while he was writing his best pastoral novels), once we are entirely beyond its influence in the last pages of *Jude the Obscure*, a magic pall falls over Hardy. Death stalks the pages in a most bizarre way. The great malignant unmoral Nature seems to wither his brain. He can only groan again and again that we are victims. There is no more green time of seasons, harvests, generations, fathers, and sons—only the timelessness of the grotesque child who is no child. A false beginning without even a significant end, Little Father Time may truly be seen as an allegory of the death of pastoral green time. However tough-minded Hardy's long love affair with the pastoral may occasionally seem, when even its faintest breath has gone, Hardy is clearly destitute. Having, as she thinks, cut beyond all conventional form, Sue falls back exhausted from her Ishmaelitish heroism to cling to the most banal conventions.

We must, however, acknowledge Sue's complex attractiveness to Hardy—as a woman surely, even as a Venus Urania or a Shelleyan ideal (cf. 253). But ultimately she is most *interesting* to him as the apotheosis of "modernism." At the end of the novel Hardy mourns not only the pathos of Jude's failure with Oxford and Sue, and not only the death of the pastoral (beyond the winter death and vernal rebirth possible in green time), but the death of a pastoral that deserves to die, that could not endure the last of a long series of tests by various visions of the modern. It is almost as though Hardy needs only one glance at Sue with her shepherd's crook mouthing her version of pastoral "freedom" to send him forever from the English novel.

To epitomize this portrait of modernism in Sue, Jude's description of her as "so ethereal a creature," "uncarnate" (207) provides the best clue—my comments on her epicureanism another. Some emptiness has slipped between consciousness and feeling, between mind and will, between form and substance.

> "Some women's love of being loved is insatiable; and so, often, is their love of loving; and in the last case they may find that they can't give it continuously to the chamber-officer appointed by the Bishop's license to receive it." (225)

A "love of being loved" and a "love of loving" are so reminiscent of Eustacia's epicureanism that we need not argue the point here (see also 264 for Sue's "love of being loved"). But Sue has rendered the very emotion "uncarnate." Somewhere amidst all Sue's passion for "being loved" and "loving," the specific love of Jude has been bled white.

She adopts Little Father Time after having induced in Jude a denunciation of the incarnation of parent in child that Jude rather admires for all its tragic potential. (He mourns at one point that Sue's children by Phillotson, should there be any, will be only half Sue.)

> "What does it matter, when you come to think of it, whether a child is yours by blood or not? All the little ones of our time are collectively the children of us adults of the time, and entitled to our general care. That excessive regard of parents for their own children, and their dislike of other people's, is, like class-feeling, patriotism, save-your-own-soul-ism, and other virtues, a mean exclusiveness at bottom." (297)

No doubt Hardy sympathizes with Jude's speech here, but Jude has tailored it to Sue's enthusiasm for the "uncarnate": she responds immediately by jumping up and kissing Jude with "passionate devotion" (297). Hardy and Sue and Tess and any number of Hardy's characters can be excused for wanting to purge the inheritance of parents and ancestors from children, so dark and apparently cursed are their bloodlines. Yet, however much a child may suggest that he is born of a *Zeitgeist*, he nonetheless has a human father and mother whose qualities, as Hardy well knew, are somehow incarnate in him. To make the father of Little Father Time so abstract may be a

psychological necessity for Hardy as for Jude, but for the reader it is a remarkable instance of Sue's influence (in a not entirely undesirable way)
working on Jude.

The child himself is characterized by an innate talent for reversing the
general tendency of children to "begin with detail, and learn up to the general; they begin with the contiguous, and gradually comprehend the universal" (301).

> The boy seemed to have begun with the generals of life, and never
> to have concerned himself with the particulars. To him the houses,
> the willows, the obscure fields beyond, were apparently regarded
> not as brick residence, pollards, meadows; but as human dwellings
> in the abstract, vegetation, and the wide dark world. (301)

It has never been observed that this innate ability to uncarnate everything
specific and tangible is very much like Sue and is a great affinity between
them. Little Father Time, however, is always regarded as Hardy's distilled
essence of the modern apocalypse, while Sue is not usually seen in this
way. In a very demonstrable sense, then, Sue is the spiritual mother of Little Father Time.

When Sue later says, "It is strange, Jude, that these preternaturally
old boys almost always come from new countries" (303), she is revealing
Hardy's sense that the kind of unnatural oldness represented by this child
is antithetical to the sense of the past Hardy had cultivated so carefully in
his long use of the pastoral and local antiquity. This contrast between the
two crucial senses of the past is beautifully visualized by Hardy in an image where Little Father Time, floating in his "morning-life" on the ocean of
time, is borne up occasionally by a "groundswell from ancient years of
night," "when his face took a back view over some great Atlantic of Time,
and appeared not to care about what it saw" (299). As in Hardy's poem
about the "journeying boy" on a train, "Midnight on the Great Western,"
the appropriate question for modern man as for Little Father Time is,
"What past can be yours?" Little Father Time does not know, as the poem
says, "whence he came"—he does not know who his mother is, and he has,
with considerable symbolic importance, been raised in that "new country"
with little European past, Australia. One defining quality of the modern
sensibility for Hardy is that, knowing in an abstract way a good deal about

the past, it cannot really possess a past: "What past can be yours?" Our fatal flaw is that like the boy we can see a great Atlantic of the past and not "care" about its content. This view of time is truly the bane of pastoral green time. It is an image permeated by the futility of time.

We may construct a ladder of proportions by way of describing the danger in Sue's sensibility: as the trap is to the rabbit, so marriage has been and may be again to both Sue and Jude (234); so social forms of all sorts are to the free spirit; and so the incarnate form of any ideal thought or feeling is to the "uncarnate" (for example, the specific love of tangible Jude to a love of "loving" and "being loved"). Thus the theme of her Ishmaelite rebellion against "played out" forms extends upward toward a disdain for the specific of anything as against its ideal.[5] As Tess would have, Jude promptly makes his way downstairs and kills the trapped and suffering rabbit with one blow. Sue is "so glad you got there first" (235).

One wonders how far Sue's ability in producing the uncarnate really is from this:

> "He had the faith—don't you see?—he had the faith. He could get himself to believe anything—anything. He would have been a splendid leader of an extreme party." "What party?" I asked. "Any party," answered the other.

We are still a long way (though only two years in actual time) from Marlow's description of that great prophet of modernism, Mr. Kurtz: "Hollow at the core." But in Sue it is just possible Hardy has set the course that genuinely leads into the modern heart of darkness. No one denies that Sue feels tremendous guilt at the death of Little Father Time and her own children, and that this guilt drives her to comply with the "forms" she had so proudly violated. In some sense of the word she still loves Jude as he goes coughing off into the rain. But she needs even more her own penance, ostensibly for having precipitated the suicide and murders but more profoundly (in Hardy's subtlest understanding of her role) for violating that vision of form and function and substance, of spirit and body, the perfect incarnation so vividly conveyed in the symbol of the sheep-shearing barn in *Far From the Madding Crowd*. She is, I suppose, very much a creature of her transitional time and place, whose mission as a character is to bring the spirit of "uncarnation" to a culture whose illegitimate incarnations are increasingly repressive and apparent. But as she and Hardy and Jude come to see, neither love nor civilization can be based on the spirit of "uncarnation"; in that sense she is truly civilization's "negation" and most assuredly the negation of the declining pastoral perspective that Hardy had tried almost mystically to extend in Tess. She does not imply a future. Like Little Father Time, she is the end of time: all civilization, any civilization must posit its forms of incarnation just as a lover must love another human individual and not the idea of "loving."

Surely Robert B. Heilman is right when he summarizes his careful description of Sue's incredible array of inconsistencies and contradictions as a "turmoil of emotions [that] will not let the mind, intent on its total freedom, have its own way."[6]

> In all ways she is allied with a tradition of intellect; and she is specifically made a child of the eighteenth century. She dislikes everything medieval, admires classical writers and architecture, looks at the work of neo-classical secular painters, conspicuously reads eighteenth-century fiction and the satirists of all ages. Jude calls her "Voltairean," and she is a devotee of Gibbon. She is influenced, among later figures, by Shelley as intellectual rebel, by Mill's liberalism, and by the new historical criticism of Christianity. (221–22)

For Heilman, Sue's failure implies "the danger of trying to live by rationality alone" (Heilman, 222) as well as her and Jude's inability to see that conventions embody, however inadequately and repressively, the attempt of civilization to incarnate the life of the emotions and unreason. Reason dismisses conventional forms as a "needless constraint" (223), but Sue's words invariably "betray the split between reason and feeling, between the rational critique of the forms and the emotional reliance on them" (224): "Hardy shows that her emotions cannot transcend the community which her mind endeavors to reject" (225). This "community," however, is far more than "the forms of feeling developed by the historical community" (226), and the modernity in Sue is more than the peculiarly modern "threat of intellect to the life of feeling and emotion" or even the implications of "warnings against arid rationality, and visions of a reconstructed emotional life essential to human safety and well-being" (226) that Heilman rightly sees in such prophets of the modern situation (if I may supply some names) as W. B. Yeats and Freud.

Despite the accuracy and uncanny comprehensiveness of Heilman's portrait of Sue, the community at stake must be that larger consonance of form and substance and function that reverberates throughout Hardy's versions of the pastoral and that finds its apotheosis in Tess. Sue completes the extraction of Jude from far more than the social forms he is inclined to respect, leaving him (as she herself is) adrift with what D. H. Lawrence was to call a rootless "conceit of consciousness." She and Oxford finally draw him from those primal sympathies which lie at the basis of "community" understood in the largest pastoral sense; and that is the full dimension of Sue's modernity. Jude's incredibly dark apprehension of man's fate at the end of this novel is the perspective of unsupported mind, deprived of any human community that links men with a viable past and with social forms that at least acknowledge the great irrational substratum of all existence— deprived above all of those great ontological channels between the human and the nonhuman worlds. All the horrible things that Sue says to Little Father Time, things that partly cause the suicide and murders, seem overwhelmingly true to this sort of isolated intellect. Severed from the emotions and sexuality that Sue would etherealize, her intelligence can only see Nature's law as "mutual butchery" (333). Oddly enough, although she is willing to take responsibility for having said things that tip Little Father Time over the edge, she cannot see that her unsupported and consequently wildly erratic and contradictory intellect has just as surely completed the ruin of Jude. Not only Sue, however, but the whole modern situation suffers from this devolution of mind away from its deepest ontological roots. If Sue herself is uncarnate, Hardy suggests that consciousness itself has become so.

A crucial element in this portrait of rationality is that Nature and some form or conception of society have come to reflect each other in Hardy's imagination, as they always have in the tradition of the pastoral. It is as though Nature's law is "mutual butchery" not because reason has finally seen the reality of things, but because Nature is no longer viewed from the perspective of community. Without a usable past and social forms that do justice to the "nonhuman" aspect of human character that D. H. Lawrence sought, Nature itself becomes somehow alien. As with Lawrence, Hardy strongly senses that we either feel these larger-than-human forces running through us or we are compelled to see them as totally other, victimizing us with their indifference. Both Edward Tylor and Frazer had pointed out a similar grasp of alternatives in the "primitive" mind. From the perspective of Tess, however flawed and tenuous or even tragic it may be, these very faults of Nature, natural selection itself, can occasionally seem to rise toward a higher sense of community which has been the true subject of all pastoral. In the Garden of Eden, as Milton and a large part of the Christian renaissance pastoral tradition saw it, the ideal community of man, woman, and God embodies the ideal relation with Nature. All these relations are inseparable in the symbolic sense that community or society involves psychological, sexual, and cosmic hierarchies.

In the ideal pastoral world, even when the author shows us Nature's tempests and brings the disturbance of "yearning for what one cannot possess" into the green world (as Virgil usually did),[7] man's society sees itself as mediated by larger internal psychological and external cosmic societies. The idea that our view of Nature depends on the kind of society from which we view it has an incalculable symbolic importance, not only for understanding Hardy's novels but for the entire late-Victorian and Edwardian cosmology. There are no important Victorian or Edwardian writers for whom the issues of man's place in the new universe and the disintegration of society are not somehow joined, to the degree that the one becomes inevitable metaphor and symptom of the other. In a strictly homocentric sense, of course, Hardy would say that regardless of our society's form or condition, the new science will still have revealed the Darwinian struggle and man as an accident. But Hardy knew that cosmological truth was in the highest sense no more autonomous than the "faculty" of reason itself—that both operate properly only in the kind of total vision or myth that only integrated societies and more-than-homocentric points of view produce. Much as a survival survives the mythopoeism that bore it and gave it fullest life and is in search of a society, of a new mythology that will once more give it sustenance, so even if the "truth" of Jude's and Sue's view of man's place in Nature is, for Hardy, logically irrefutable, it does not follow that there is no larger ontology that can master it. It is unfortunately true that there is nothing in Jude's poor collection of cultural fragments or in Sue's extreme deracination that can do so. The new Darwinian Nature becomes totally dark and unbearable only when there is no imaginative conception of a whole society from which to view it—or, to be more precise, only when questions of educational reform or marriage contracts and questions of Nature's process seem unrelated.

Here we are very close to the ultimate affinity between Hardy and D. H. Lawrence, at least as that connection truly exists and not as Lawrence saw it. Sue reminds us of those characters in Lawrence who, though of course no longer under the aspect of the great Miltonic hierarchies that make every psychological observation in *Paradise Lost* at once societal and cosmic, are nonetheless related to the Lawrencian sense of the "organic" as against the "mechanical." Hermione of *Women in Love*, for example, describes passionately how reason, analysis, self-consciousness, and, in vague summary, "mind" poison the deep wells of intuition, instinct, "body," the sense of our original connections with Pan. As Lawrence's characters devolve toward one extreme or the other—toward Hermione's violation of the whole man (called "man alive" by Lawrence), or toward increasingly sensuous distortions—Lawrence's ideal of the harmonious man ("mind" and "dark body" linked to produce true "spirit") continually asserts that these distortions within each "man alive" all have their implications for society and our view of the cosmos. Birkin verbally lashes Hermione and accuses her of having no desire for "the dark sensual body of life" except through "the worst and last form of intellectualism, this love of yours for passion and the animal instincts."[8] Very much like Sue, Hermione "loves" passion with her will and intelligence and "conceit of consciousness, and [her] lust for power, to *know*" (46). Sue, uncarnate consciousness that she is, also lives with the fearfully intensified will that Lawrence identified with the distortions of the whole "man alive" in either direction, toward either form of fragmentation. The implications of Sue's devolution and distortion for the improved society that Hardy sought are no less powerful, say, than the implications of Gerald's contrary devolutions for the world of the collieries: Gerald reduces his workers to their "instrumentality," and Gudrun, watching him sleep, sees him

> sheerly beautiful. He was a perfect instrument. To her mind, he was a pure, inhuman, almost superhuman instrument. His instrumentality appealed so strongly to her, she wished she were God, to use him as a tool. (476)

These disharmonies in the "man alive" produce characters who some-times feel like a particularly instrumentalist God: Gerald toward his work-ers ("And Gerald was the God in the machine" [260]), and Gudrun toward her Gerald, and ultimately Loerke toward his Gudrun. A related distortion in Sue is surrounded no less by death and, we may say in conclusion, im-plies no less a cosmos and society determined to dehumanize its people, to prevent them from being the harmonic ideal of "man alive." Of Sue we may say, as Birkin does of Hermione, "Passion and the instincts—you want them hard enough, but through your head, in your consciousness. It all takes place in your head, under that skull of yours" (45).

Although no writer really parallels Lawrence, his taste for the "non-human, in humanity" (which "is more interesting to me than the old-fashioned human element") points to a similar concern in Hardy for hu-man character as an aspect of forces that have made the entire cosmos. The letter to Edward Garnett that includes the famous reference to the "non-human" ties Lawrence's casual denunciation of the old-fashioned concep-tion of ego rather precisely to swift intellectual forces of the time, to "fu-turism" and Schopenhauerian Will certainly.[9] The whole letter, though its argument is rather beneath the surface, offers not Freudian complication for the new "ego" but a distinctly Hardian feeling for character that reaches out to the stars and down to the buried ruins and fossils for the essence of discrete egos. But of ego, it must be noted, no less poignant and significant for being linked with forces other if not greater than man. Even the "futur-ists," who look for the "phenomena of the science of physics" in human character, are almost saved in Lawrence's eyes by their sense that man is part of natural and not divine forces larger than man. We are more nearly in the world of *Wuthering Heights* than that more characteristically Victo-rian world of *Middlemarch*. For Lawrence in *Women in Love*, not only in-dividual characters but all of Western civilization stands or falls in its rela-tion to these forces. If, as George Ford cogently argues, *Women in Love* is thus a great "war" novel, *Jude the Obscure* may at least be seen as a prelimi-nary blast on the ram's horn.[10]

In bringing Jude to Oxford and then to Sue, Hardy had been bringing his own battered and deprived pastoral sensitivity to the gates of reason, learn-ing, and urban culture, to the "conceit of consciousness." Like Oxford's, Sue's portals are effectively closed to him. Hardy's and Jude's remnant of rustic sensibility, far from discovering its fulfillment in the life of reason, finds there an overwhelming sterility. Neither Sue nor Oxford can do for the pastoral remnant what Hardy's imagination did: preserve its life and all its difficulties pending the vision which can unite it with the potentially life-giving rational qualities—the qualities that, for all their failings, make both Oxford and Sue the legitimate objects of Jude's love. There may be a new symbolic building for the modern world which is neither one of Jude's Gothic churches nor Sue's railway station, nor even Somerset's addition to the Castle de Stancy in *A Laodicean*. Until it is built, Sue's unfettered reason will be like an architectural detail awaiting the comprehensive design that can give it meaning. Against the oceanic formlessness of Little Father Time's image, however, the hope emerges only fitfully that our society will make something equivalent to what the ancient British earthwork of Mai-Dun was to its culture or the great sheep-shearing barn was to its pastoral world. Meanwhile, Hardy will conserve West Knighton and Jude will lovingly trace the Gothic carvings with his fingers, not as symbols of spontaneity and freedom, but—as a Christian might agree—of incarnation.

What Hardy has created in Sue, then, is some definitive failure of the phenomenological sensitivity that inheres in the pastoral sense of "community." To "uncarnate" reason is to so fragment man that, as in D. H. Lawrence, it is to "unprinciple" him, to do violence to his nature and to court the sort of death and cultural failure that stalks *Women in Love*. To reject the willfulness that grows apace, as Lawrence says, when man is in one way or another unprincipled, is to create the humility that allows one to feel the true correspondence, and that not in a Wordsworthian or transcendental way, but in the cold dawn of late-Victorian science. Hardy has imagined in Sue an attempt to grant the ontology of reason a dominion it cannot possibly support. The result is the haunting image of Sue as the false shepherd, an allusion that must confirm our speculations about the phenomenological bent of the whole pastoral tradition as Hardy uses it. The alternatives in Hardy's work seem to be the phenomenological sensitivity that may restore ancient senses of community and allow us to know what men and things are beyond or beneath the wrenchings of human will, and, on the contrary, a state of consciousness very much like Elizabeth-Jane's after Henchard has nearly "unprincipled" her in his habitual fashion. Elizabeth-Jane joins the world of things in not knowing why she is one thing rather than another; she is helpless, yearning for "release" from the

question of identity entirely. If consciousness has a future, Hardy intimates, it must be toward "aletheia," toward discovery of its own nature
within larger cosmic ontologies—and that not at all to the defeat of individual personality.

In his *Literary Notes* Hardy often meditated on the contribution of Herbert Spencer (especially in *Principles of Biology*, 1864) to Hardy's faith
that, as Spencer argued, "It cannot be said that inanimate things present no
parallels to animate ones."[11] This continuity of consciousness with "lower"
forms of life and finally with matter itself (in its most dynamic and evolutionary aspect) is, let there be no doubt, the very keystone of Hardy's art
viewed phenomenologically. It is an impulse that one must take into account not only in *The Dynasts*, where it surfaces so conspicuously, but in
Hardy's taste for William Kingdon Clifford's answer to the question "What
is Consciousness?" Clifford argued that elementary feelings can exist without what humans recognize as consciousness, and that since elementary
feelings can be traced down to the simplest organisms, although "a moving
molecule of inorganic matter does not possess mind or consciousness," it is
nonetheless the "mind-stuff" of all feeling on up past the point where feeling becomes self-consciousness. On this mind-stuff, Hardy wrote to Roden
Noel in 1892:

> You may call the whole human race a single *ego* if you like; and in
> that view a man's consciousness may be said to pervade the world;
> but nothing is gained. Each is, to all knowledge, limited to his own
> frame. Or with Spinoza, and the late W. K. Clifford, you may call all
> matter mind-stuff (a very attractive idea this, to me) but you cannot
> find the link (at least I can't) of one form of consciousness with
> another.[12]

Although community (this "link"), was not to be found in the bare
quasi-scientific idea of mind-stuff, the phenomenological point of view, la-
boriously achieved in his novels, did allow Hardy to see the nonhuman in
the human. This is the same vision that so impelled D. H. Lawrence's work
and, for reasons that emerge from the spirit of the time, so much of early
modern art. What Hardy could not achieve in scientific ideas or rather
threadbare philosophy, his imagination—working through an ancient genre
equally dedicated to finding the link—could achieve in the great pastoral

novels. As Walter Wright says, Hardy was ready to entertain John Morley's claim in *Diderot and the Encyclopaedists* that "man has become as definitively the object of science as any of the other phenomena of the universe."

> Hardy would not, of course, go nearly so far, but underlying Morley's argument was a belief in an identification of the nature of man with certain characteristics of the universe. Morley was not saying that to follow Nature was good; such a view would have aroused Hardy's scorn. But Hardy could concur in a search for cosmic unity.[13]

The distinction between the following Nature and perceiving man's involvement with "certain characteristics of the universe" is vital. We are accustomed to seeing Hardy as the great cosmic pessimist for whom consciousness is almost a curse, a means of perceiving our victimage in the cogs of an impersonal scheme that does not take man into account. And that much he often is, even in the course of his greatest art. But he was equally a natural phenomenologist who could sense in the nonhuman world the modes of consciousness itself and who, unlike Joseph Conrad finding a common denominator of undifferentiated blackness behind all being, could detect a strange community in which the fossil trilobite, human consciousness, and the tall forests themselves undulate to ancient pastoral notes. In even his ethical cry of victimage and indignation, we may detect another note: that Hardy knows how much of even that ethical indignation is sheer anthropocentrism. There is in Hardy's greatest work a profoundly moving sense that ours are not the only standards in the universe, that the world was subjected to other scrutiny and other feelings for eons before man came on the scene to assume his Jobian posture. The pathos and indignation of the ethical view are less Hardy's true timbre than the slightly muted oaten strain. Beyond the injustice of it all lies a state of mind where justice is not the question. This view, it must be recognized, is a good deal different from theories which speculate that Hardy may have surmised a creative evolution, the great unconscious will moving agonizingly toward eventual consciousness. On the contrary, I see this emphasis on the parity of all life and on the significance of the nonhuman in the human as a brilliant antidote to anthropocentrism; will, whether understood in a Schopenhauerian or more ordinary sense, is less the creative impulse than the bane of Hardy's ideal consciousness. We are all "to be with the small," and in life as well as in death.

Notes

Introduction

1. J. Hillis Miller, in one of the first phenomenological studies of literature ever attempted by an American critic, applied Husserl's methods to Hardy in *Thomas Hardy: Desire and Distance* (Cambridge: Harvard University Press, 1970). His method had less to do with bracketing a text than with the description of Hardy's *Lebenswelt* and with the intentionality in the consciousness producing that Lebenswelt. Edward Said's study of Joseph Conrad can properly be called the first substantial phenomenological study in English of an English novelist: *Joseph Conrad and the Fiction of Autobiography* (Cambridge: Harvard University Press, 1966). Though influenced by Miller, Heidegger, and Sartre, Said followed the lead of continental phenomenological critics such as Roland Barthes, who considered that the method demanded the critic's own subjective meditation and the blurring of novel with letters and life in order to detect essential structures of the author's project toward the world. Said, in his article, "Roads Taken and Not Taken in Contemporary Criticism" (in *Contemporary Literature* 17, no. 3 [Summer 1976]: 327–48), describes in detail the origins of his phenomenological approach and its relation to poststructuralism and so-called deconstructionism. The article is a brilliant summary of the interest contemporary phenomenological critics take in the whole problem of "textuality." Said's version of phenomenological method shows its greatest weakness in Peter J. Glassman's book, *Language and Being: Joseph Conrad and the Literature of Personality* (New York: Columbia University Press, 1976), where the ontological status of the "text" is so confused that Husserl's original insights seem to have been oversimplified nearly out of existence. To many current phenomenological critics in America, the method seems to consist primarily of challenging the privileged status of the text, largely in the manner of Stanley Fish, who himself holds no special brief for phenomenology. Husserl himself saw no difference between the lived experiences, *Erlebnisse*, of, say, a mathematical proposition or a tree on one hand and a fictional character or even an entire fictional text on the other. His philosophy makes no room for special theories of "textuality," though it should be apparent that some of these, Fish's for instance, could be turned on Husserl's own texts with fascinating results.
2. I use the translation by W. R. Boyce Gibson originally published in 1931 and available in paperback, Collier Books, through Macmillan, London (1962). Page references are to that edition. I also read the original German, and some of my comments are based on that trying experience.

3. W. B. Yeats, *A Vision* (New York: Macmillan, 1956), pp. 83–84.
4. Wylie Sypher, *Loss of the Self in Modern Literature and Art* (New York: Random House, 1962).
5. Particularly in *Logische Untersuchungen*, 1900, and *Ideen* I, 1913.
6. See Adaline Glasheen, *Third Census of Finnegans Wake* (Berkeley: University of California Press, 1977), p. lxxii and following chart.
7. D. H. Lawrence to Edward Garnett, June 5, 1914, *Collected Letters of D. H. Lawrence*, ed. Harry T. Moore (New York: Viking, 1962), 1: 281–82.
8. *The Woodlanders*, pp. 59, 245. Unless otherwise noted, quotations and page references are from the Wessex Edition (London, 1912–31).
9. Christine Winfield, "The Manuscripts of Hardy's Mayor of Casterbridge," most conveniently seen in the Norton *Mayor of Casterbridge,* ed. James K. Robinson (New York: Norton, 1977), pp. 269–70.
10. William Barrett, *Time of Need: Forms of Imagination in the Twentieth Century* (New York: Harper & Row, 1972), pp. 72–76.
11. Barrett, p. 74.
12. Ibid.

Chapter One. *Far From the Madding Crowd*

1. Hallett Smith, "Elizabethan Pastoral," in *Pastoral and Romance: Modern Essays in Criticism*, ed. Eleanor Terry Lincoln (Englewood Cliffs, N.J.: Prentice-Hall, 1979), p. 18. Since so many of the key modern comments on the pastoral are in this handy anthology, I have often referred to it. The extract is from Hallett Smith, *Elizabethan Poetry* (Cambridge, Mass.: Harvard University Press, 1952). Richard Cody in *The Landscape of the Mind: Pastoralism and Platonic Theory in Tasso's "Aminta" and Shakespeare's Early Comedies* (Oxford: Clarendon Press, 1969) has an interesting allegorical interpretation of the Golden Age which considerably deepens our understanding of otium as a psychological state.
2. Michael Squires in *The Pastoral Novel: Studies in George Eliot, Thomas Hardy, and D. H. Lawrence* (Charlottesville: University of Virginia Press, 1974) does this nicely, especially in chapter 5.
3. Renato Poggioli, "The Pastoral of the Self," p. 53, in *Pastoral and Romance*.
4. All page references to Hardy's novels are in parenthesis in the text and refer, unless otherwise noted, to the 1912–31 Wessex Edition.
5. Patricia Hutchins, "Thomas Hardy and Some Younger Writers," *Journal of Modern Literature* 3, no. 1 (1973): 35–44.
6. Jean R. Brooks, *Thomas Hardy: The Poetic Structure* (Ithaca, N.Y.: Cornell University Press, 1971), pp. 172–74.

7. Virgil, *Works*, rev. ed., 2 vols., trans. H. Rushton Fairclough (Cambridge: Harvard University Press, 1950), 1:43.
8. H. J. Lose, *The Eclogues of Vergil* (Berkeley and Los Angeles: The University of California Press, 1942), pp. 94–104.
9. Rita Ransohoff, "Sigmund Freud: Collector of Antiquities, Student of Archeology," *Archeology* 2, no. 28 (April 1975): 108.
10. T. R. Southerington, *Hardy's Vision of Man* (New York: Barnes and Noble, 1971). The Idea permeates the book, without, however, an adequate basis being laid for it in Hardy's exploration of the pastoral.
11. Poggioli, p. 53.

Chapter Two. *The Return of the Native*

1. Because of its interesting textual note, I have used the Houghton Mifflin Riverside Edition, edited by A. Walton Litz (Boston, 1967) in this chapter. This is based upon the 1912 Wessex Edition with, of course, different pagination.
2. "Shall Stonehenge Go?" in *Thomas Hardy's Personal Writings*, ed. Harold Orel (Lawrence, Kansas: University of Kansas Press, 1966), pp. 196–201.
3. See Marvin Harris, *The Rise of Anthropological Theory* (New York: Thomas Y. Crowell, 1968), especially pp. 164–68.
4. Harris, p. 164. E. B. Tylor and his *Primitive Culture* are mentioned in a passage from Herbert Spencer's "Last Words about Agnosticism and the Religion of Humanity," *The Nineteenth Century* 16 (November 1884): 828–29, a passage that Hardy summarized, annotated, and partly quoted in his notebook of *Literary Notes*. See *The Literary Notes of Thomas Hardy*, ed. Lennart A. Björk, 2 vols. (Goteborg, Sweden: Gothenburg Studies in English, 1974), vol. 1, text 1336. Volume 1 consists of two separately bound books, Text and Notes. The item discusses fetishism, one of Hardy's favorite subjects and certainly one that turns up frequently in passages that Hardy quoted and annotated from Comte for his *Notes*. Spencer quotes Tylor in support of his theory that a fetish derives its potency from a prior belief in ghosts and spirits, though he rather ironically refers to Tylor as a man "who has probably read more books about uncivilized peoples than any Englishman living or dead." As anthropologists were soon to insist, reading books about primitive peoples was not the best way to know them.
5. See Harris, p. 201.
6. For all this see *Literary Notes*, 1: notes 669, 618, 620, 882, 1336, and indeed the entire matrix of relations between Hardy's interests in Comte and Spencer as suggested by the *Literary Notes*.
7. Harris, pp. 166–67.

Chapter Three. *The Mayor of Casterbridge* and *The Woodlanders*

1. Matthew Arnold, *Lectures and Essays in Criticism*, ed. R. H. Super (Ann Arbor: University of Michigan Press, 1962), p. 230. Quoted by Hardy in his *Literary Notes*, 1:note 1018 (see note 4, chapter 2, for full documentation).
2. D. H. Lawrence, *Phoenix*, 2 vols. (London, 1968), 2:227.
3. John Paterson, "Lawrence's Vital Source: Nature and Character in Thomas Hardy," in *Nature and the Victorian Imagination*, ed. U. C. Knoepflmacher and G. B. Tennyson (Berkeley: University of California Press, 1977), p. 462.
4. This and other such comments are scattered throughout Florence Emily Hardy, *The Early Life of Thomas Hardy* (London: Macmillan, 1928) and *The Later Years of Thomas Hardy* (London: Macmillan, 1930), e.g., "October 2. Looked at the thorn bushes by Rushy Pond [on an exposed part of the heath]. In their wrath with the gales their forms resemble men's in like mood."
5. Ernest Brennecke, Jr., *Thomas Hardy's Universe: A Study of a Poet's Mind* (London: T. Fisher Unwin, 1924), especially pp. 18–25.
6. Mercea Eliade, *Myth and Reality* (New York: Harper & Row, 1963), chaps. 1 and 2.
7. J. O. Bailey, *Thomas Hardy and the Cosmic Mind: A New Reading of "The Dynasts"* (Chapel Hill: University of North Carolina Press, 1956), p. 13.
8. Bailey, pp. 12–13.

Chapter Four. *Tess of the d'Urbervilles*

1. My page references are to the Norton Critical Edition, ed. Scott Elledge (New York: W. W. Norton & Company, 1965), which is essentially the 1912 Wessex Edition collated with the 1895 edition that included Hardy's revisions of the novel's first publication in book form.
2. Although it is customary to conjure up Hardy's intellectual background by reference to William R. Rutland, *Thomas Hardy: A Study of His Writings and Their Background* (Oxford: Russell and Russell, 1938; New York, 1962), Perry Meisel's criticism of that exposition is superb in his *Thomas Hardy: The Return of the Repressed* (New Haven and London: Yale University Press, 1972). Meisel's sensitivity to Darwin is unmatched among recent critics of the Victorian novel, although one need not agree with his final analysis of Hardy according to a subtly revised sense of Darwin's impact. See especially Meisel's "Introduction."

3. David Lodge, *Language of Fiction* (New York: Columbia University Press; London: Routledge and Kegan Paul, 1966), pp. 176–88. David Lodge's essay, "Tess, Nature, and the Voices of Hardy," along with others by Dorothy Van Ghent and David DeLaura that I mention subsequently, are conveniently collected in *Twentieth Century Interpretations of "Tess of the d'Urbervilles,"* ed. Albert J. LeValley (New York: Prentice-Hall, 1969).

4. David J. DeLaura, "'The Ache of Modernism' in Hardy's Later Novels," *ELH* 34, no. 3 (September 1967): 380–99.

5. Dorothy Van Ghent, *The English Novel: Form and Function* (New York: Holt, Rinehart & Winston, 1953), pp. 195–209.

6. Quoted by the editor along with other selections from Florence Emily Hardy's *The Early Life of Thomas Hardy* and *The Later Years of Thomas Hardy* in *Twentieth Century Interpretations*, p. 107.

7. Elliot B. Gose, Jr., "Psychic Evolution: Darwinism and Initiation in *Tess of the d'Urbervilles*," *NCF* 18 (1963): 261–72.

8. *The Early Life of Thomas Hardy* (London: Macmillan, 1928), p. 294.

9. *The Origin of Species: A Variorum Text*, ed. Morse Peckham (Philadelphia: University of Pennsylvania Press, 1959), p. 172. Darwin later changed this to read "whole community."

10. Stanley Edgar Hyman, *The Tangled Bank: Darwin, Marx, Frazer and Freud as Imaginative Writers* (New York: Atheneum, 1962), pp. 26–30. Indeed the whole first chapter of Hyman's book is required reading. Although this book should have been widely influential, it was and is still unknown by many who should know it best.

11. If the reader is interested in Conrad's sometimes peculiar notions about the ethical value of survival qualities, he might look at my "Conrad's 'Falk': Manuscript and Meaning," *MLQ*, 26 (June 1965): 267–84. Many of Conrad's changes in the manuscript of "Falk" indicate a deepening interest in whether the strongest was also in some sense the "best."

12. Hyman makes something like this point throughout his discussion of Darwin, but especially on pp. 39–40. See Darwin himself in the Variorum Text, e.g., p. 162, line 165.

13. Hyman, p. 41.

14. Hyman, p. 42.

15. *Collected Poems of Thomas Hardy* (New York: Macmillan, 1953), p. 527.

16. Meisel, p. 56.

17. Meisel, p. 60.

18. Meisel, p. 66.

19. Meisel, quoting D. H. Lawrence in "Study of Thomas Hardy," in *Selected Literary Criticism*, ed. Anthony Beal (New York, 1969), p. 67.

20. Harold E. Toliver, *Marvell's Ironic Vision* (New Haven: Yale University Press, 1960). This and following quotations are all from pp. 88–89.
21. See the context provided for this quotation in F. B. Pinion, *A Hardy Companion: A Guide to the Works of Thomas Hardy and Their Background* (New York: St. Martin's, 1968), pp. 103–4.

Chapter Five. *Jude the Obscure*

1. Page references are to F. R. Southerington's edition of *Jude the Obscure* (Indianapolis and New York: Bobbs-Merrill, 1972), as the most satisfactory edition available.
2. *The Architectural Notebook of Thomas Hardy*, ed. C. J. P. Beatty (Dorchester, Dorset: Dorset Natural History and Archaeological Society, 1966). I am greatly indebted to Beatty's "Introduction," from which all quotations in these two paragraphs are taken.
3. From Florence Emily Hardy, *The Later Years*, p. 23. See Beatty, p. 34.
4. Robert Gittings, *Young Thomas Hardy* (Boston and Toronto: Little, Brown, 1975), p. 4.
5. See also p. 239: "Sue's logic was extraordinarily compounded, and seemed to maintain that before a thing was done it might be right to do, but that being done it became wrong; or in other words, that things which were right in theory were wrong in practice."
6. Robert B. Heilman, "Hardy's Sue Bridehead," in *Hardy: The Tragic Novels*, ed. R. P. Draper (London: Macmillan, 1975), pp. 209–26. The Heilman essay originally appeared in *NCF* 20 (1965–66). This quotation is from page 224, and subsequent page references are given in parentheses in the text.
7. Harold E. Toliver, *Pastoral Forms and Attitudes* (Berkeley: University of California Press, 1971), pp. 1–2, n. 1.
8. *Women in Love* (New York: Random House, Modern Library, 1950), p. 45. Subsequent page numbers refer to this edition.
9. D. H. Lawrence to Edward Garnett, June 5, 1914, *Collected Letters of D. H. Lawrence*, ed. Harry T. Moore, 2 vols. (New York: Viking, 1962), 1: 281–82
10. George H. Ford, *Double Measure* (New York: Norton, 1965), chaps. 8, 9.
11. *Literary Notes*, 1: note 882. See note 4, chapter 2 for full documentation.
12. *Literary Notes*, 1: note 1215.
13. Walter Wright, *The Shaping of "The Dynasts": A Study in Thomas Hardy* (Lincoln: University of Nebraska Press, 1967), p. 36.

Index

Abraham, 61
Abstention. *See Epokhē*
Achilles, 39
Aletheia, 7, 153
Altruism, 115, 116
Anahuas or Mexico and the Mexicans, Ancient and Modern (Tylor), 62
Analysis of Gothic Architecture (Brandon), 135
Ancient Law (Maine and McLennan), 64
Anthropocentrism, 154
Anthropologists. *See* Evolutionary anthropologists
Anthropomorphism: in Hardy's novels, 5–6. *See also* Nature
Aphrodite, 32, 33, 34
Architectural metaphors, 22, 29–30, 33, 103, 152. *See also* Gothic architecture
Architectural Notebook (Hardy), 135
Aristotle, 12
Arnold, Matthew, 76, 112, 129
Artemis, 42
Aspiring mind: components of, 10; in characters and compared to otium, 10, 22, 43, 46, 68–70, 73, 91, 94, 137; Hardy's view of, 122

Bachelard, Gaston, 1, 7
Bacon, Francis, 10
Ball, Cain, 21
Barn. *See* Sheep-shearing barn
Barrett, William, 6, 7
Bathsheba. *See* Everdene, Bathsheba
Baudelaire, Charles, 36
Beatty, C. J. P., 136
Being and Nothingness (Sartre), 3–4

Berenson, Bernard, 56
Bible, 16, 32
Blake, William, 95, 129
Boldwood, William: relationship with Bathsheba, 15, 25, 26, 29, 34, 45, 46; description of, 25–26; disjunction of, 34; murders Troy, 45
Brandon, Raphael, 135
Brennecke, Ernest, 84
Bridehead, Sue, 43, 44, 53, 76, 108, 125, 129, 136; modernism of, 139–40, 143–44, 146–48; primitiveness of, 140; marriage to Phillotson, 140, 141; relationship with Jude, 140–41, 142, 152; as an Ishmaelite, 141, 142, 143, 146; estrangement from nature, 141–42, 143, 146, 148; devolution of, 148, 150; compared to Lawrence characters, 150–51
Brontë, Charlotte, 15, 16
Brontë, Emily, 49, 53–54

Camus, Albert, 31
Carlyle, Thomas, 137
Cervantes, 11, 43
Chain Salpae, 19, 20
Charmond, Mrs., 84, 86, 89
Christianity: Hardy's view of, 29, 99, 103, 108; decline of, 29–30, 32; and paganism, 31, 32, 76, 97–99, 101–2, 118, 130, 138; evolution of, 63; in modern world, 67; restraints of, 112
Christminster. *See* Oxford
Clare, Angel, 125; relationship with Tess, 6, 102, 103–4, 105, 107–8, 109, 110, 111, 112, 117, 118, 119, 122; taste for "newness" of, 106, 107, 109, 110, 117, 118, 119, 122; faith of, 107, 108;

dox of, 81, 83; as Elizabeth-Jane's
father, 82–83; death of, 83
Henchard, Susan, 77, 79, 81, 82
Hercules, 16, 17
Hirsch, E. D., 2
Horizon-collapsing images, 26, 48
Howards End (Forster), 96
Hughes, Ted, 118
Husserl, Edmund, 1, 2, 3, 4, 6, 7, 8, 47,
128
Huysmans, 36
Hylas, 16, 17, 28, 33, 34
Hyman, Stanley Edgar, 116, 118–19,
122

Idealism. *See* Philosophic Idealism
*Ideen zu einer reinen Phänomenologie
und phänomenologischen Philo-
sophie* (Husserl), 1, 46–47
Iliad, The, 39
Immanent Will, 8, 80, 88, 98, 115, 116,
151
Individualism. *See* Self-identity
Ishmael, 61, 69, 83, 141, 142, 146
Isolation, 20, 60

Jane Eyre (Brontë), 14, 15, 16
Joyce, James, 2, 4, 67
Jude. *See* Fawley, Jude
Jude the Obscure (Hardy), 84, 90, 91,
112, 126, 129–54

Kant, Immanuel, 6, 47
Knight, Henry, 123–25, 127

Laodicean, A (Hardy), 76, 136
Late Lyrics and Earlier (Hardy), 121
Lawrence, D. H., 3, 4, 6, 8, 13–14, 15–
16, 22, 23, 31, 37, 42–43, 46, 67, 68,
78, 85, 109, 112, 126, 148, 150–51,
152, 153

*League of the Ho-de-no-sau-nee, or
Iroquois* (Morgan), 64
Lévi-Strauss, Claude, 79
Linnaeus, 134, 135
Literary Notes (Hardy), 62, 63, 64, 65,
153
Little Father Time, 142, 143, 144–45,
146, 147, 148, 152
Logical Investigations (Husserl), 2
Lord Jim (Conrad), 7, 8
Lose, H. J., 33
Lubbock, John, 62–63, 64
"Lycidas" (Milton), 18, 28, 29
Lyell, Sir Charles, 65, 98

McLennan, J. F., 64
Maid's Tragedy (Beaumont and
Fletcher), 45
Mai-Dun, 152
Maine, H. S., 64
Marlowe, Christopher, 10, 146
Marriage, 79–80, 129, 142–43, 150
Maumbury Ring, 60
Max Gate, 76
Mayor of Casterbridge, The (Hardy),
5, 66, 76–94
Meisel, Perry, 123, 125, 126
Melbury, Grace, 5, 100; relationship
with Winterborne, 77, 90–91; re-
bellion against society, 85; relation-
ship with nature, 85, 89, 92, 93–94;
Fitzpiers returns to, 86–87
Melville, Herman, 61
Middlemarch (Eliot), 151
"Midnight on the Great Western"
(Hardy), 145
Milgate, Michael, 76
Mill, John Stuart, 138, 147
Miller, J. Hillis, 1
Milton, 10, 16, 17, 28, 29, 50, 149, 150
Modernism: Hardy as transitional fig-